THE ACTIVE READER

An Introductory Reading/Communication Text
for Students of ESL

CHRISTINE PEARSON CASANAVE

Stanford University

DIANE WILLIAMS

Monterey Institute of International Studies

 PRENTICE HALL REGENTS, Englewood Cliffs, New Jersey 07632

Library of Congress Cataloging-in-Publication Data

CASANAVE, CHRISTINE PEARSON, 1944-
    The active reader.

    Includes index.
    1. English language—Text-books for foreign
speakers. I. Williams, Diane, 1956- . II. Title.
PE1128.C434 1987   428.2'4   86-25528
ISBN 0-13-003740-0

Editorial/production supervision and
    interior design: Virginia Rubens
Cover design: Diane Saxe
Manufacturing buyer: Carol Bystrom
Illustrations: Christine Pearson Casanave

© 1987 by Prentice Hall Regents
Prentice-Hall, Inc.
A Paramount Communications Company
Englewood Cliffs, New Jersey 07632

Printed in the United States of America

10 9

ISBN 0-13-003740-0

9 780130 037404

90000

PRENTICE-HALL INTERNATIONAL (UK) LIMITED, *London*
PRENTICE-HALL OF AUSTRALIA PTY. LIMITED, *Sydney*
PRENTICE-HALL OF CANADA INC., *Toronto*
PRENTICE-HALL HISPANOAMERICANA, S.A., *Mexico*
PRENTICE-HALL OF INDIA PRIVATE LIMITED, *New Delhi*
PRENTICE-HALL OF JAPAN, INC., *Tokyo*
PRENTICE-HALL OF SOUTHEAST ASIA PTE. LTD., *Singapore*
EDITORA PRENTICE-HALL DO BRASIL, LTDA., *Rio de Janeiro*

Contents

CHAPTER 8 Having Fun *166*

Teacher's Introduction

Summary of Important Points

- Students' extensive background knowledge and experience needs to be activated for reading to be meaningful and efficient.

- Decoding vocabulary and grammar is not the same as reading.

- Good readers monitor their own reading comprehension, integrate what they read with what they know, and make predictions from text.

- Students in ESL classes need opportunities to share their knowledge and opinions and to respond to exercises that are open-ended as well as "right or wrong."

- Language growth occurs when students interact meaningfully with their peers, with native English speakers, and with print.

The Active Reader is an introductory reading/communication text for young adult and adult ESL students who plan to use English as a medium for study and work. By "introductory," we mean that *The Active Reader* is designed to be used by these students as a first textbook in the American classroom. The communication activities help students get to know each other, in addition to serving as a foundation for reading by activating background knowledge and providing vocabulary on each topic. The topics deal with issues that are likely to concern newly arrived students and that they will be familiar with through experience. The level of language in the text can be broadly described as high-beginning. While the writing is simple, we have made no attempt to control the vocabulary and syntax artificially or formulaically.

The text has eight chapters. All eight can be covered in a ten-week quarter. By taking full advantage of the communicative aspects of the text, teachers can stretch it into a fifteen-week semester. Each chapter begins with extensive communicative prereading activities and with a brief survey of the main reading article. The main reading article is then presented twice—once interpolated with questions designed to help students monitor their comprehension and make predictions, and once uninterrupted. Reading strategy exercises and additional readings that vary in length and genre follow the main reading. Each chapter concludes with The Word Section, which consists of word-level exercises. Vocabulary and topics are recycled in each chapter's exercises and additional readings. Vocabulary is further recycled from chapter to chapter. The chapter readings and exercises increase in difficulty and length as the book progresses. Notes to the teacher and suggested answers to many of the exercises appear in a separate Teacher's Manual.

In the remainder of this introduction, we present a more detailed description of and rationale for the main features of *The Active Reader*.

Prereading Activities

The communicative prereading activities in *The Active Reader* ask students to organize and express their own knowledge on each chapter's broad theme. Many of the activities have students interact with each other; others ask them to seek information outside class from native English speakers. In all cases, as well as through a brief survey of each main reading article, students activate their existing knowledge, practice key vocabulary, and focus on specific issues and themes.

By emphasizing the importance of communicative prereading activities in this text, we hope to convey our belief that reading is not just a process of decoding vocabulary and syntax, but of interacting meaningfully with a text. Such interaction can take place only *after* students have a basic grasp of the topic and vocabulary of the reading. If they must struggle with both new language and new topics during the reading process, then reading as we understand it is not taking place.

Main Reading Article: An Introduction to Comprehension Monitoring, Integrating, and Predicting

In order to tap students' background knowledge, which is triggered by the prereading activities, and to assist students in monitoring their comprehension as they read, we have incorporated into the first presentation of the main reading a series of paragraph-by-paragraph questions. These questions ask students to reflect on their understanding of what they have just read, to consider it in light of what they already know, and, based on this understanding, to think ahead to what they may be reading in the next paragraph or section. In the second half of the text, we ask students to take on more responsibility for monitoring their own comprehension. Several paragraphs are presented uninterrupted, and questions reflect inter-paragraph issues. In the last chapter's main reading, no questions appear; students are only reminded to check their comprehension on their own. (Note: Teachers may wish to read aloud the "By Paragraph" reading so that students can make necessary sound-symbol correspondences.) All main readings are then followed by a full uninterrupted version, intended to be read silently and quickly, and a set of broad comprehension questions.

We have approached the reading task this way because we believe that such an approach reflects effective reading strategies. In our native language, the processes of checking, monitoring, taking corrective action when something goes wrong, fitting what we read into our existing knowledge systems, and predicting come quite naturally to the proficient reader. When we read in a foreign language, however, and when our students read in English, our monitoring processes break down, especially if we are reduced to word-by-word decoding. We do not process large chunks of text easily, nor do we think to stop periodically to ask ourselves whether and what we have understood.

It is especially important, then, for beginning readers in a foreign language to bring to the reading task all possible strategies to make reading easier. Reliance on vocabulary and syntax is not sufficient. We encourage teachers to continue this broad strategic approach as they help students work through the additional readings in each chapter.

Exercises, Further Readings, and The Word Section

Exercises in each chapter help students become aware of some basic strategies that can improve their reading. Recognizing pronoun referents is practiced in every chapter. Other exercises include recognizing grammatical word groups, distinguishing facts and opinions, ordering information, recognizing levels of generalization, and agreeing or disagreeing with statements related to each chapter's topic. In The Word Section, further exercises give students practice with selective reading, finding analogies, making word associations, and understanding word forms. It is hoped that teachers will incorporate some of these skills and strategies into their treatment of the additional readings.

Like the communicative prereading activities, some of the exercises in *The Active Reader* ask students to use each other, as well as native speakers outside the class, as resources. We encourage student–student and student–native speaker interaction whenever possible in the belief that it promotes growth in the second language and acculturation to the target culture. Furthermore, one way that we acquire deeper understanding of what we read, and solve both school- and work-related problems, is to consult with others. Numerous open-ended exercises and discussion questions promote such interaction and allow for individualized responses as well.

From two to five additional readings are included in each chapter. While the vocabulary and general theme are chapter-related, individual readings vary greatly in length and genre. Short "telegraphic" readings include a wedding invitation, a telegram, memoranda, and instructions. Longer readings include a letter, historical and biographical readings, and readings on culture shock (an American perspective), buying medicine, and the play of animals. In most chapters, one of the additional readings is considerably more challenging than the others.

Each reading is followed by thought-provoking questions that are intended to help students make inferences and form opinions from what they read. "Display" type questions are avoided. The questions are meant to be discussed by two or more individuals, though they could also be given as homework. We believe that difficult but necessary skills in both first and second language reading involve learning to risk making inferences and refining the logic of our interpretations. With the cognitively mature second language reader, it is never too early to begin this practice.

Other Issues

Directions

The directions and explanations to the exercises and activities should be considered reading matter. However, especially in the early chapters, they will probably be too difficult for students to understand fully on their own. Teacher and students can best work through directions and explanations together. (Further suggestions to teachers appear in the Teacher's Manual.)

Small Group Work

If students have not worked in small groups in a classroom situation before, they may need explanation and practice before this arrangement feels proper. If students and/or teacher are not comfortable with group work, most of the activities can be carried out in the traditional teacher-fronted manner.

Contact Assignments

Whenever appropriate, we recommend that teachers arrange to have students consult with native speakers outside the ESL class. Students will need to be prepared with some gambits that will allow them to open, explain, and close an encounter appropriately. Shy students might complete contact assignments in pairs. If contact assignments outside class are not feasible, the teacher might invite friends and colleagues to participate in small-group activities inside the class. Regardless of how the contact assignments are conducted, students should be encouraged to solicit information from native speakers orally. It might be tempting for some to simply hand a native speaker a worksheet with instructions to fill it out. Students will need to understand the importance of the contact assignments for their overall language development.

Timed Readings

Timed readings are not included in *The Active Reader*. Because the readings are not comparably difficult and vary significantly in terms of length and genre, we felt that timing reading and charting "progress" were not appropriate.

Testing

If it is necessary to give tests, we recommend that teachers clearly distinguish tests of reading from tests of vocabulary, grammar, memory, and so on. A reading test might consist of one of the additional readings and its inference questions, or a comparable teacher-made passage. Such a reading test would need to look at the reading passage globally as well as locally, to ask students to bring their own knowledge and opinions to the text, and perhaps to relate issues in the text to something else they had read or experienced.

Conclusion: The Reader's Contribution

Finally, we believe that each reader brings unique experiences and knowledge to the reading task. These nontext factors influence in part how readers interpret what they read. What prevents totally idiosyncratic interpretations of text, or course, must be features in the message of the text itself. But these text-bound features can be interpreted *only* in the light of what each reader brings to the text. Our young adult and adult ESL reading students bring an astonishing, and often unrecognized, richness of experience to the ESL classroom. Whether or not we plan for it, this background knowledge provides the foundation for their understanding of what they read and experience in the United States. What many ESL reading textbooks fail to take advantage of is this richness of individual experience in the second language reading process.

It is our hope that students, with the helpful reminders of teachers, will actively bring what they know to the reading task *and* monitor their comprehension as they read. We further hope that teachers will encourage students to work together on exercises and on comprehension and discussion questions. It is not our intention to lead students to "the right answer." Rather, we hope that together, with each other and with their teacher, they will discover that reading is a kind of problem-solving that becomes enriched through a flexible, open-ended discussion, in which individual contributions are valued rather than evaluated and criticized.

Acknowledgments

We would like to thank the following people for their assistance in the development of this book: Mimi Corneli, Pat Hall, Jan Thoele, and the ESL students at the Monterey Institute of International Studies; Robin Baliszweski, Brenda White, and Virginia Rubens at Prentice-Hall; and our friends and relatives, all of whom have been patient and supportive.

To the memories of Arnita and Colleen, two strong women who inspired me.

CRPC

To my parents, who first taught me to love reading.

DW

LIST OF ABBREVIATIONS AND SYMBOLS

n	noun
v	verb
adj	adjective
adv	adverb
prep	preposition
pn	pronoun
expr	expression; idiom
sing	singular
pl	plural
C	countable noun
U	uncountable noun
=	*means; is*

CHAPTER 1

Getting Acquainted

GET-ACQUAINTED ACTIVITIES

Part 1   Names, Names, Names!

What is your teacher's name? What are your classmates' names? Where are they from? This get-acquainted activity will help you learn this information.

Step 1:   Preparations

You need one index card (or 1/4 piece of notebook paper). Write this information on the index card:

Full name (first name and family name): <u>e.g.* *Nobuko Segawa*</u>

Name you wish to be called in class: <u>*Nobuko*</u>

Home city/country: <u>*Kyoto, Japan*</u>

A distinguishing characteristic:** <u>*glasses*</u>

---

*e.g. = for example

**a distinguishing characteristic = something that people can observe about you

Here are some examples of distinguishing characteristics:

glasses

blue shirt

blue eyes

bald

brown pants

tall

striped skirt

short

round face

jogging shoes

long face

bracelet

big nose

Note: Some of the characteristics are permanent (e.g., physical characteristics). Other characteristics are temporary (e.g., clothing).

Each student needs a card, and the teacher needs one, too. Here is an example of a card for Nobuko:

```
Nobuko Segawa

Nobuko

Kyoto, Japan

glasses
```

Step 2:   Put all of the cards into a paper bag (or a box, or a hat). Mix up the cards.

Step 3:   Distribute one card to each student and one to the teacher. (You should not have your own card.)

Step 4:   Find the person on your card. (Note: You will need to walk around the classroom. Ask: "Are you [Nobuko]?")

   If the person answers "No," ask his or her name; give your name. Then keep looking for the person on your card.

   When you find the person, put a check (✔) on the card. KEEP THE CARD. Review the information on the card. Make sure that it is all correct. Then return to your seat.

Step 5:   When everyone is finished, introduce the person on your card to the class: "This is Nobuko. She's from Japan." Can you remember everyone's name? Practice the names in class. Try to use names every day.

Part 2 Book Survey

In the last activity, you got acquainted with your classmates and with your teacher. In this section, you will get acquainted with this book. You will see how the book is organized. You will learn some special vocabulary. Here is some of the vocabulary that you will practice:

title	chapter	page	paragraph
prereading	article	key word	exercise
directions	table of contents	survey	

Now, answer these questions with your teacher and classmates.

1. What is the **title** of this book? _____

2. How many **chapters** are in this book? _____

3. What is the title of Chapter 3? (Hint: Look in the **table of contents.**)

   _____

   Chapter 7? _____

4. How many **pages** are in this book? _____

5. Look at Chapter 2. Find the following sections. Write the first page number of each section on the line:

Section	*Page Number*
Prereading Activities	_____
Reading Article	_____
Exercises and Further Readings	_____
The Word Section	_____

6. Question 5 asked you to look at Chapter 2. Do other chapters have the same sections?   Yes ☐   No ☐

   In other chapters:

   a. Which section comes first (1st)? _____

b. Which section comes second (2nd)? _____

c. Which section comes third (3rd)? _____

d. Which section comes fourth (4th)? _____

7. The prefix *pre-* means *before*. What does *prereading* mean?

_____

In this book, the prereading activities prepare you to read the main reading articles. These activities give you the topic and some of the vocabulary of the articles.

There are two kinds of prereading activities. The first kind is a communication activity. In the communication activity, you will often talk with your classmates. You will share your knowledge with them, and they will share their knowledge with you. In the second kind of prereading activity you will **survey** the chapter to see what it is about. To survey an article or a chapter is to look at it quickly to get a general idea about it.

8. Look at Chapter 2 again. Find the reading article. The reading article is presented two times:

The first time, the reading article is divided into **paragraphs**. There are some questions after each paragraph. The questions help you understand each paragraph. They also prepare you to read the next paragraph.

The second time, the reading article is divided into the same paragraphs, but there aren't any questions until the end of the article. You can read the complete article without stopping.

9. Look near the end of the Prereading Activities in Chapter 2. Find the list of words. These are **key words**. A key word is an important word. The key words in the list are important words in the reading article. You can learn something about the reading article by reading the list of key words.

10. Find the *Exercises and Further Readings* Section in Chapter 2. Each exercise begins with **directions**.

a. Read the directions for one of the exercises.

b. Where can you find directions (in general)? (Check one.)

At the beginning of an exercise. ☐

In the middle of an exercise. ☐

At the end of an exercise. ☐

c. Is the word *instructions* similar to the word *directions*? Ask a classmate or your teacher if you are not sure.

Yes, similar. ☐   No, different. ☐

11. How many exercises are in the following chapters? (Do not include READ.)
   a. Chapter 2: _____
   b. Chapter 4: _____
   c. Chapter 8: _____

12. How many extra readings are in the same chapters?
   a. Chapter 2: _____
   b. Chapter 4: _____
   c. Chapter 8: _____

13. Find *The Word Section* in Chapter 2. What are the names of the exercises in this section?

   _____

   _____

   _____

   _____

14. You have now completed a **survey** of this book. You know a little about what is in the book. Put a check (✔) next to each activity that you will probably do in each chapter of this book:

   _____ communicate with classmates

   _____ communicate with people outside class

   _____ read an article paragraph by paragraph

   _____ memorize grammar rules

   _____ learn about words

   _____ read a complete article

   _____ read a newspaper

   _____ read directions

   _____ read a map

   _____ write compositions

   _____ write answers to exercises

   _____ survey each chapter

   _____ listen to a tape from each chapter

   _____ read several extra articles

Part 3   Introduction to the Exercises

In this section you will learn how to do the exercises in this book. Most of the exercises are in the section called *Exercises and Further Readings*. A few are in a section called *The Word Section*. One exercise (Predicting; see **A.** below) is from the *Prereading Activities* section. Each exercise has a different name. The names of the exercises are special vocabulary words. You will learn these words little by little. You do not need to memorize them now. It is more important to learn how to *do* the exercises.

A.   *Predicting*

Predicting is guessing about a future event. When you read, you can sometimes predict what the writer will say next. Predicting can make reading easier for you.

In this book, some questions appear after some of the paragraphs in the main reading article. Some of the questions ask you to THINK AHEAD. To predict is to think ahead—to guess about what is coming next in the reading article. Let's look at an example. Read the following sentence. Imagine that it is the first sentence of a paragraph:

My hometown is beautiful.

What do you think the author (= the writer) of this sentence will write next? ____

a. information about his or her family

b. a description of his or her hometown

c. a description of famous people in his or her hometown

Did you choose letter *b*? Letter *b* is the best answer. Why? (Hint: Look at the word *beautiful*.)

Let's look at another example. Read this sentence:

Reading is important for all educated people.

What do you think the writer will tell us next? ____

a. reasons why reading is important

b. a description of educated people

c. ideas about the importance of writing

Which answer did you choose? Why? (Letter *a* is the best answer. Look at the subject of the sentence—reading; look at the word *important*.)

Predicting is a useful skill in reading. If we can think ahead—guess what a writer is going to tell us in the next sentences and paragraphs—then we can understand what we read more easily.

Now, practice making predictions. Read each sentence. What will the writer probably tell us next? Choose the best "next sentence."

1. Each chapter in this textbook has four sections. ____
   a. There are several kinds of exercises in the third section.
   b. The sections are Prereading Activities, Reading Article, Exercises and Further Readings, and The Word Section.
   c. This textbook has eight chapters.

2. My classmates are from several different countries. ____
   a. My classmates and I are studying English.
   b. Different countries have different systems of government.
   c. These countries include Japan, Mexico, Indonesia, Saudi Arabia, Switzerland, and China.

3. It is important for teachers and students to learn each other's names. ____
   a. English-speaking people have a first name, a middle name, and a last name.
   b. Sometimes names are difficult to pronounce.
   c. By learning names, teachers and students will feel comfortable with each other.

B. *Selective Readings*

The Selective Reading exercises are easy and fun. Their purpose is (a) to give you practice moving your eyes quickly from left to right (left → right); (b) to help you see words quickly; and (c) to help you think in terms of categories, topics, and examples. In these exercises you will **select** (choose) one or more words from a line, and circle, underline, or cross out your choices. Let's practice.

1. *Directions:* Cross out the words in the line that are different from the word in parentheses.

   (book)   book   book   hook   look   book   took

   Did you cross out three words? (hook, look, and took)

2. *Directions:* Cross out the word in the line that does not belong in the group.

book   magazine   newspaper   television   letter

Did you cross out the word television? Can you explain why it does not belong in the group?

3. *Directions:* Underline all of the number words in the sentence.

When I did the exercise the first time, I did not understand questions four, seven, and nine, but the second time I understood everything.

Did you underline five (5) words? Which ones?

4. *Directions:* One word in the line is a general category word. The other words are examples of the category. Circle the category word.

first name   name   nickname   last name   middle name

Which word did you circle? Can you explain why?

As you can see, these exercises are easy. You should try to do them quickly, and if possible, explain your answers. You have learned several important vocabulary words: **cross out, underline, circle, category,** and **example.**

C. *Grammatical Word Groups*

A **grammatical word group** is a group of words that go together in a grammatical way.

EXAMPLE: a small book

This grammatical word group consists of a determiner (*a*), an adjective (*small*), and a noun (*book*). But look at the next group:

EXAMPLE: a small blue

This group of words is not a complete grammatical word group. It has a determiner, two adjectives (*small* and *blue*), but no noun. We ask ourselves: A small blue *what*? We don't know the answer.

We can understand the meaning of what we read more easily if we read in grammatical word groups. As you become more familiar with English grammar, it will be easier for you to read in grammatical word groups.

In this book, there are two kinds of grammatical word group exercises. In the first kind, you need to identify grammatical word groups. In the second kind, you need to read them. Let's practice both kinds:

1. *Directions for the first kind of exercise:*   Underline all of the grammatical word groups that are the same kind as the group in parentheses.

   (to read)   to study   of students   to the store   to listen

   EXPLANATION: The group in parentheses consists of the preposition *to* and a verb. This grammatical word group is called an **infinitive phrase.** There are two infinitive phrases in the line: *to study* and *to listen.*

Here's another example:

   (in the book)   to write   for the teacher   in the class   on the desk   the book
   is blue   my notebook

   EXPLANATION: This time, the group in parentheses consists of a preposition (*in*), a determiner (*the*), and a noun (*book*). It is called a **prepositional phrase.** How many prepositional phrases did you underline? (There are three.)

2. *Directions for the second kind of exercise:*   The following paragraph is divided into grammatical word groups. Read the paragraph as quickly as you can.

It is important
for teachers and students
to learn
each other's names.
By learning names,
students and teachers
will feel comfortable
with each other.
Classmates
will enjoy talking
with each other.
Students
will not be afraid
to speak in class.

Here is the same paragraph printed with normal spacing:

It is important for students and teachers to learn each other's names. By learning names, students and teachers will feel comfortable with each other. Classmates will enjoy talking with each other. Students will not be afraid to speak in class.

In this book, we will sometimes ask you to practice reading in grammatical word groups. Do sentences in your language divide easily into grammatical word groups? Do you read in grammatical word groups in your own language?

D. *Order*

When we talk about **order,** we are talking about a sequence of ideas or items: what comes first, second, third, and so on. Look at these examples of order:

Alphabetical Order	*Numerical Order*	*Chronological Order*
a, b, c, d, e, . . .	1, 2, 3, 4, 5, . . .	1984, 1985, 1986, 1987, . . .

Most reading material has some kind of order. If we can understand how the sentences and ideas are ordered, we can read more easily. In the order exercises, you need to read groups of sentences and decide which sentences should be first, second, third, and so on. Here's one for you to try:

Directions: Put a number in front of each sentence to show the best order.

_____ Then I have breakfast.

_____ At 4:00 I go home and take a nap.

_____ I get up at 7:30 a.m.

_____ I study at school until 4:00.

_____ After that I go to school.

Now, read the sentences in the correct order. You can see that the sentences go together in a logical way to make a story. What kind of order is demonstrated in the sentences?

_____ alphabetical order

_____ numerical order

_____ chronological order

E. *Reference*

There are many kinds of reference, but in this book we will mostly practice one kind—pronoun reference. Read the following sentence:

They study English.

This is a perfectly good sentence. Unfortunately, we do not know who *they* are! The pronoun *they* refers back to people who were mentioned in a previous (earlier) sentence:

My classmates are from many countries. They study English.

Now we know that *they* refers back to *my classmates* (a noun phrase). The pronoun reference ties the two sentences together.

THEY = MY CLASSMATES

If you see personal pronouns in a sentence, you know that these words refer back to an earlier noun phrase.

EXAMPLES OF PERSONAL PRONOUNS: *it, he, she, they, him, her, them*

In the following sentences, the pronouns are underlined. They refer back to a noun phrase. Can you find the noun phrase?

1. Most students bring paper and pencils to class. Sometimes <u>they</u> bring pencil sharpeners and erasers, too.

    THEY = _____

The pronoun *they* is plural. Therefore, you need to find a plural noun phrase. There are two plural noun phrases in the first sentence: *students* and *pencils* (or *paper and pencils*). But only one of the noun phrases makes sense as a referent for *they*. Why? (What is a logical subject for the verb *bring*?)

2. Each chapter has a reading article. First <u>it</u> is presented paragraph by paragraph. Then <u>it</u> is presented without interruption.

    IT = _____
    IT = _____

In this group of sentences, *it* appears two times. Does it refer to the same noun phrase? Which one? *Each chapter* or *a reading article*? (Use your knowledge of chapters and reading articles to decide.)

3. Professor Newhouse is going to give the class five quizzes this term. <u>She</u> plans to give <u>them</u> on Fridays.

SHE = _____

THEM = _____

Can you understand the second sentence without the information in the first sentence? No. You need to know that *she* refers to the teacher and *them* refers to the quizzes.

4. Professor Newhouse has many students from Asia in her classes. <u>She</u> has never visited <u>there</u>, but hopes to go next summer.

SHE = _____

THERE = _____

In these sentences, the word *there* is an adverb, not a pronoun. It refers to a location (a place)—Asia.

F. *Levels of Generalization*

We can divide a topic into parts according to **levels of generalization**—general, specific, and more specific. For example, if our topic is engineering, we can divide it this way:

GENERAL: engineering

SPECIFIC: electrical engineering, mechanical engineering, civil engineering

If our topic is computers, we can divide it this way:

GENERAL: computers

SPECIFIC: microcomputers

MORE SPECIFIC: Apple, IBM, Kaypro. . .

When we read, we need to understand the levels of generalization of the writer's ideas. In other words, we need to identify a topic, then find examples and details of that topic. By understanding how a writer divides a topic, we can understand a writer's ideas more clearly. The exercises in this section help you think about the levels of generalization of a topic.

Directions: Read the group of words. Write **G** before the **general** word. Write **S** before the **specific** word. Write **MS** before the **more specific** word. Then read the words in the order **G, S, MS.**

1. ___ sentences

   ___ paragraphs

   ___ words

2. ___ adjectives

   ___ small, red, new

   ___ words

   You can see from items 1 and 2 that words are general or specific only *in relation to each other.* In number 1, *words* is **MS.** In number 2, *words* is **G.** The same is true, of course, for sentences and ideas. Let's try an example with sentences.

Directions: Write **G** before the *general* sentence, **S** before the *specific* sentence, and **MS** before the *more specific* sentence. Then read the sentences in the order **G, S, MS.**

3. ___ They come from Europe, Asia, and Latin America.

   ___ Students come to the United States from all over the world to study
   English.

   ___ Professor Newhouse, for example, has students from France, Korea, and
   Venezuela.

   Can you explain your answer?

G. *Analogies*

An **analogy** is a similarity or a correspondence between two things. In most of the analogy exercises in this book, an analogy will be presented as a *ratio: "Book* is to *read* as *television* is to *watch."* We can write this as:

   book : read   television : watch.

The relation between *book* and *read* is similar to the relation between *television* and *watch*. We read books; we watch television.

This type of analogy exercise is fun. Here are some examples:

Directions: Look at the analogy. Complete it with a word from the line of words.

1. adjective : blue   noun : _____

  red   small   interesting   car   quickly

2. _____ : sandwich   drink : Pepsi

  lunch   eat   buy   good   large

3. market : food   _____ : books

  library   study   read   office   cafeteria

Sometimes writers use analogies in order to express an idea. For example, the following sentence expresses an analogy:

Learning a language is like cooking.

You, the reader, need to figure out how language learning and cooking are analogous (similar or parallel). With several classmates, make a list of the ways in which language learning and cooking are similar.

H. *Fact or Opinion*

When we read, we sometimes need to understand the difference between a **fact** and an **opinion.** A fact is something that actually happened, something that is true. An opinion is someone's personal idea about something—for example, about whether something is good or bad.

  EXAMPLE 1: **Prime Minister Indira Ghandi was assassinated in 1984.**

    Fact ☐   Opinion ☐

This is a fact, because the event actually happened. But:

  EXAMPLE 2: **Indira Ghandi was a good prime minister.**

    Fact ☐   Opinion ☐

This statement is an opinion. Some people believe very strongly that she was a good prime minister. Other people believe very strongly that she was not.

Sometimes we confuse facts and opinions. It can be very difficult to distinguish the two. Therefore, the fact and opinion exercises in this book will cause some discussion. Discussion is good in these exercises. Try these examples. Talk about your answers.

1. English is becoming an international language.

   Fact ☐   Opinion ☐

2. English is an easy language to learn.

   Fact ☐   Opinion ☐

3. John F. Kennedy was a good president.

   Fact ☐   Opinion ☐

4. Ronald Reagan was elected President of the United States two times.

   Fact ☐   Opinion ☐

I.   *Agree/Disagree*

The agree/disagree exercises will help you make and express opinions about something that you read. It is not necessary for you to agree with everything that you read. In fact, if you plan to attend an American university, it will be important for you to have opinions about what you read. It is also important for you to explain your opinions so that other people can understand your point of view.

There are no "right" answers to the agree/disagree exercises. Your answer is correct because it is yours. However, you should try to defend (explain, justify) your answer. There will be a lot of discussion with this exercise.

Directions: Read the statements. Do you agree or disagree with them? Discuss your answers in class.

1. Everyone should study English.

   Agree ☐   Disagree ☐

2. American food is bad.

   Agree ☐   Disagree ☐

3. It is necessary to understand every word in a reading article.

   Agree ☐   Disagree ☐

J. *Making Inferences*

What is an inference? An **inference** is an educated guess. Look at the following example. The first sentence is known information. The second sentence is an inference from the known information.

Sentence 1—Known Information: **Yoshi has not eaten anything yet today.**

Sentence 2—Inference: *Yoshi is probably hungry.*

Notice that Sentence 1 does not tell us that Yoshi is hungry. We guess (infer) that he is hungry. Here is another example:

Sentence 1—Known Information: **This school has a large program of English as a Second Language (ESL).**

Sentence 2—Inference: *A lot of foreign students attend this school.*

Sentence 1 does not tell us that there are a lot of foreign students at the school. We use our knowledge of ESL programs to make an inference about the number of foreign students.

Good readers are able to make inferences from what they read. They use their knowledge of a topic and of the kind of material they are reading in order to make inferences. It is necessary for readers to make inferences because writers do not tell readers everything. Writers give clues to readers. They expect readers to use these clues and their own knowledge to understand the reading material.

In this book, you will practice making inferences from extra readings. These readings are at the end of the Exercise section. Some questions follow each reading. You cannot find the answers to all of the questions directly in the reading. You must make inferences from the reading in order to answer the questions. Let's practice.

Directions: Read the selection. Then answer the inference questions.

October 16
Dear Mother,

School began last month. I have been very busy. I'm sorry I didn't write sooner. I hope that you and Father are well and not angry with me.

I have a nice roommate. She is from Japan. We are in the same English class. We have class six hours every day, and then we go to a language laboratory and listen to tapes. When I get home I am exhausted. I just want to sleep. The classes are not difficult, but speaking and listening to English all day makes me so tired. I understand only about 50 percent. My pronunciation is terrible—other people don't understand me when I talk.

I have to repeat myself many times. Everybody tells me that I will improve quickly. I hope so.

Well, I have a lot of homework to do. For tomorrow I have grammar exercises and a composition to write. Please give my love to everybody in the family. I promise to write again soon!

Love,

Graciela

Answer the questions. The answers are not stated directly in the reading. You must use the reading *and* your knowledge to make inferences.

1. What kind of reading material is this? ____
   a. a newspaper article
   b. a letter
   c. a chapter from a book

2. Who wrote it? ____
   a. the mother
   b. a teacher
   c. a student

3. Graciela hopes that her mother and father are not angry with her. Why does she think they might be angry?

   _____

4. What is Graciela studying? _____

5. Do you think that Graciela has been at her school for a long time or a short time?

   _____

6. What did Graciela probably do on the evening of October 16?

   _____

Now go back and look at your answers. What information and knowledge did you use in order to find your answers?

Concluding Remarks

By now, you are acquainted with your classmates and your teacher. You are also acquainted with this book. But at the present time, you don't know your classmates or this book *well*. After a few weeks, both your classmates and this book will be familiar to you, and you will feel comfortable with them.

Here are a few things to remember:

- You have a lot of knowledge (about life, about people, about your field of interest). Use this knowledge when you communicate with your classmates and when you read.

- Talking in English will help you remember vocabulary.

- Doing the exercises in this book will help you remember vocabulary and will acquaint you with some basic reading skills.

- You do not need to understand every word in every reading article in order to understand ideas from a reading article. You can understand a lot even if you know only 50 percent of the words.

- Writers do not tell readers every detail about a topic. Often you need to guess, or to use your own knowledge when you read.

- You learn to read, in part, by reading. You need to read as many things in English as you can: newspapers, stories, letters, advertisements, labels, and, of course, this book!

HAVE FUN BECOMING AN ACTIVE READER!

CHAPTER 2

Goodbyes and Promises

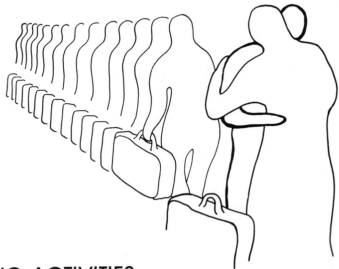

PREREADING ACTIVITIES

Part 1: Goodbyes

Who did you say goodbye to before you came to this country? Put a check (✔) in the appropriate blanks.

I said goodbye to   ____

     my mother   ____

     my father   ____

     my brother(s)   ____

     my sister(s)   ____

     my nieces and nephews ____

     my grandparents   ____

     my aunts   ____

     my uncles   ____

     my cousins   ____

my husband   ____

my wife   ____

my children   ____

my friends (female) ____

my friends (male)   ____

my teacher(s)   ____

my business associates ____

my _____

my _____

Fill in at least two of the charts.

Chart 1.   Where and how did you say goodbye to your friends and relatives? Put a check (✔) or an X in the appropriate boxes.

	At a party	At home (individually)	At the airport (train/bus station)	By phone	(Other)
Parents					
Brother(s)/ sister(s)					
Nieces/ nephews					
Grand- parents					
Aunts/uncles					
Cousins					
Husband/ wife					
Children					
Friends					
Business associates					
(Other)					

Chart 2. What do you usually do at a goodbye party with friends? With family? Put a check or an X in the appropriate boxes.

	Eat and drink	Listen to music	Talk	Sing	Dance	(Other)
With friends						
With family						

Chart 3. How do you, your friends, and your family feel when you say goodbye? Put a check or an X in the appropriate boxes. Write your own word in the "Other" column.

	Happy	Sad	Excited	Worried	(Other)
You					
Your friends					
Your parents					
Your brother(s) and sister(s)					
Other relatives					

Compare your answers with the answers of your classmates. Are your answers similar? Are some of the answers different? Talk about the similarities and differences.

Part 2: Promises

What promises did you make to friends and relatives before you left home? Put a check or an X in the appropriate boxes. (Notice how we can talk about promises: **I promised my friends to write.**)

	My parents	My brother(s) and sister(s)	My relatives	My friends
To write*				
To call**				
To eat well				
To send photos				
To study				
To spend money carefully				
To be careful				
To take care of my health				
(Other)				

Compare the promises that you made to friends and relatives with the promises that your classmates made.

a. How are your promises similar and how are they different?

b. Are the men's promises different from the women's promises?

c. Are the promises different according to country?

---

* to write (v) = to write letters

** to call (v) = to telephone

Part 3: Survey and Predict

Read the list of key words. Then look at the reading article that begins on page 32. Read the title and headings, and look at the photographs. The key words, title, headings, and photographs give you an idea about the topic* of the article. Put a check next to the topics that will probably be in this article:

_____ goodbye parties

_____ airplanes

_____ studying in another country

_____ leaving family and friends

_____ different ways to say goodbye

_____ meeting new classmates

_____ promises to family and friends

_____ studying English

_____ promises from family and friends

Key Words

to leave home	**family**	**to visit**
to say goodbye	**friends**	**a businessman**
to promise to + v	**relatives**	**to be sad (happy, wor-**
a party	**to write (letters)**	**ried, homesick, serious)**
to call (= to telephone)	**to travel**	**parents, grandparents,**
		aunt, uncle, cousin,
		niece, nephew, mother,
		father, brother, sister

---

*the topic (n, C) = the subject of an article or paragraph

Warm-up Selective Reading: Circle Same Words

Directions: Circle all of the words that are the same as the word on the left.

EXAMPLE: book: (book) back   boot   dock   hook   (book)   pool

1. say: soy   say   sag   say   sap   sad   sag   say
2. leave: leave   lean   learn   leave   leaf   learn   loaves
3. friend: fried   fiend   friend   fired   friend   friend
4. food: foot   food   food   hood   good   feet   food   fool
5. party: party   pretty   hearty   party   portly   partly
6. call: cell   sell   call   cold   salt   call   sill
7. write: write   with   rite   write   wrote   right   while

Warm-up Selective Reading: Cross Out Different Words

Directions: Cross out all of the words that are different from the word on the left.

EXAMPLE: student: study   studying   student   student   studied

1. money: money   many   money   none   monkey   more   money
2. promise: premise   promise   promise   preview   proviso
3. brother: brother   brother   bother   farther   dropper
4. feel: feet   feel   heel   feel   heat   feel   feed
5. spend: send   spend   spent   event   spend   spanned
6. parent: parent   parent   apparent   father   parent   paired

READING ARTICLE: Goodbyes and Promises

A. GOODBYES AND PROMISES By Paragraph

BEFORE YOU BEGIN: This reading is about three kinds of people: foreign students, emigrants,* and international businessmen. These people have one thing in common: they leave home, sometimes for a short time, sometimes for a long time.

1   People leave their home countries for many reasons. Foreign students leave in order to study in another country. Emigrants leave in order to make a home in a new country. International businessmen travel to foreign countries on business.

> **FROM THE ARTICLE AND FROM YOUR KNOWLEDGE:** Which of the three kinds of people in paragraph 1 are you? Or are you a different kind of person?
>
> Write your answer on the line. _____

2   All of these people have different experiences, of course, but they have some things in common. For example, they all leave familiar things behind—familiar food, familiar language, familiar people. They all say goodbye. They all make promises to friends and relatives. Let us look at three people—a foreign student, an emigrant family, and an international businessman. They will talk about their goodbyes and promises.

> **FROM THE ARTICLE:** Look at paragraph 2. Circle all the examples of the pronoun *they*. Who are *they*? ___ (Look back to the paragraph if necessary.)
>   THEY   = **a.** foreign students
>   **b.** emigrants
>   **c.** businessmen
>   **d.** all people who leave home (a, b, and c)
>
> **THINK AHEAD:** What will the rest of the article (paragraph 3 to the end) be about*? Write your idea on the line.
>
> _____
>
> _____
>
> *What is the article about? = What is the topic or subject of the article?

---

*emigrants (n, C, pl) = people who leave their countries in order to move to a new country (Compare *im-migrants*: people who come to a new country to live. The difference in the two words is in the *direction* or perspective: Emigrants *leave;* immigrants *arrive.*)

Juanita Escobar, Foreign Student

Patricia Hall

3   I came to the United States to get my Master's degree. The program at the university is two years long—a long time to be away from home!

4   Before I left home, I had a huge[1] party. I invited all of my family, friends, and relatives. My mother made my favorite foods. Everybody talked, ate, and listened to music all night. I promised to write everybody.[2] Everybody promised to write back. I think I said goodbye a hundred times. People tried to feel happy, but they were a little sad.

FROM THE ARTICLE: What is paragraph 4 about? (What is the topic/main idea?) ____
   a. a goodbye party
   b. food
   c. music

FROM THE ARTICLE: Why did Juanita leave home? ____
   a. to take a vacation
   b. to have a party
   c. to study

---

5   The next day, my parents, brothers, and sisters took me to the airport. They gave me food, vitamins, hugs, and kisses. I promised to write, to call[3] once a month, to study hard, and to take care of my health. My mother cried. My father was very serious. I think he was worried about me. The last goodbye was the most difficult.

---

[1]huge (adj) = very big

[2]to write someone (v) = to write a letter to someone

[3]to call = to telephone

FROM THE ARTICLE AND FROM YOUR KNOWLEDGE: How did Juanita's parents feel when she left home?

_____

Do you think that parents (= mothers and fathers) always feel sad and worried when their children leave home?

     Yes, always ☐   No, not always ☐

_____

THINK AHEAD: What is your prediction? We can expect the next part of the reading to be about ____ :
    a. Juanita Escobar's Master's degree program
    b. Juanita's goodbye party
    c. another kind of person who leaves home

Mr. and Mrs. Vayl and Their Son, Sasha, Emigrés

Martha Casanave

6   We left our home country a couple of years ago. We decided to emigrate because we wanted more opportunities in our lives. Nine of us came here—my wife and I, our baby (Sasha), both our parents, my brother, and my wife's sister. It was especially difficult for the old people to leave.

FROM THE ARTICLE: How many old people came to this country with Mr. and Mrs. Vayl?
    a. two
    b. four
    c. none

FROM THE ARTICLE: Who are the old people? _____

---

7   Before we left, we had a small, quiet party. At the party, we said goodbye to a few close friends and relatives. We visited other friends one by one. It was sad to say goodbye, but we promised to see everyone again in the future. We promised to write, to call, and to send everyone photographs of our new country. We promised not to forget our friends.

FROM THE ARTICLE: True or false? The Vayl family promised to return to their home country soon to visit friends and relatives.

    T   F

FROM YOUR KNOWLEDGE: Have you ever moved to a new country? Can you imagine the feelings of the Vayl family? Comment. _____

_____

---

8   We expected life to be difficult at first, and we expected to work very hard. It's difficult to get good jobs because we don't speak much English yet. My wife and I are both engineers, but right now I have a simple job as an electrician. My wife isn't working because she's pregnant. I need to find a second job.

FROM THE ARTICLE AND FROM YOUR KNOWLEDGE: What problems do people often have when they move to a new country?

_____

_____

THINK AHEAD AND FROM YOUR KNOWLEDGE: Do you think that life in the United States is easy or difficult for Mr. Vayl's parents and for his wife's parents?

Easy   ☐   Difficult   ☐

9   My parents and my wife's parents are homesick and unhappy. They don't have friends and they don't speak English. The customs, the food, and the ideas of the American people are very different. Our parents can't adjust easily. They're too old, perhaps. Life is easier for my wife and me. Even so, I wonder when I will be working as an engineer again.

FROM THE ARTICLE: Who wrote the information about the Vayl family? ____
  a. Mr. Vayl
  b. Mrs. Vayl
  c. the son, Sasha

FROM THE ARTICLE AND FROM YOUR KNOWLEDGE: Do you think that Mr. and Mrs. Vayl made a good decision to bring their parents with them to their new country? Comment.

_____

_____

THINK AHEAD: What will the last part of this reading article be about? ____
  a. a foreign student
  b. a businessman
  c. an emigrant family

Fumihiko Watanabe, International Businessman

Patricia Hall

10   I travel all the time on business, to Europe and to the United States. I don't say goodbye to my business associates because I call them every day during a business trip. In fact, I don't say goodbye to anybody except my wife and kids.[4] They aren't sad because they know that I'll return in a week or ten days. Believe it or not, they're happy when I go on a trip! I promise to bring them presents.[5] I always keep that promise. The longer the trip, the bigger the gifts!

FROM THE ARTICLE: True or false? Mr. Watanabe's wife and children are sad when he leaves home on a business trip.

        T   F

FROM THE ARTICLE AND FROM YOUR KNOWLEDGE: Mr. Watanabe buys big presents for his family when he goes on long trips. He buys small presents when he goes on short trips. Do you like this idea?

        Yes ☐   No ☐

        Comment. _____

FROM THE ARTICLE: Mr. Watanabe writes in a conversational style. He uses many *contractions (don't, I'll,* etc.). Circle all of the contractions in paragraph 10.

---

[4]kids (n, C, pl) = children (conversational)

[5]presents (n, C, pl) = gifts

Concluding Thoughts

11   In all three of the examples above,[6] people leave their home countries. They say good-bye to friends and relatives, and make different kinds of promises. For some people, leaving home is a sad experience. For others, it is a happy, exciting experience, to be repeated, they hope, many times in their lives.

B.   GOODBYES AND PROMISES   Complete Reading

1   People leave their home countries for many reasons. Foreign students leave in order to study in another country. Emigrants leave in order to make a home in a new country. International businessmen travel to foreign countries on business.

2   All of these people have different experiences, of course, but they have some things in common. For example, they all leave familiar things behind—familiar food, familiar language, familiar people. They all say goodbye. They all make promises to friends and

Juanita Escobar, Foreign Student

Patricia Hall

---

[6]above (adv) = higher on the page or on a page before this one

relatives. Let us look at three people—a foreign student, an emigrant family, and an international businessman. They will talk about their goodbyes and promises.

3   I came to the United States to get my Master's degree. The program at the university is two years long—a long time to be away from home!

4   Before I left home, I had a huge party. I invited all of my family, friends, and relatives. My mother made my favorite foods. Everybody talked, ate, and listened to music all night. I promised to write everybody. Everybody promised to write back. I think I said goodbye a hundred times. People tried to feel happy, but they were a little sad.

5   The next day, my parents, brothers, and sisters took me to the airport. They gave me food, vitamins, hugs, and kisses. I promised to write, to call once a month, to study hard, and to take care of my health. My mother cried. My father was very serious. I think he was worried about me. The last goodbye was the most difficult.

Mr. and Mrs. Vayl and Their Son, Sasha, Emigrés

Martha Casanave

6   We left our home country a couple of years ago. We decided to emigrate bec~
we wanted more opportunities in our lives. Nine of us came here—my wife an~
baby (Sasha), both our parents, my brother, and my wife's sister. It was es~
ficult for the old people to leave.

7   Before we left, we had a small, quiet party. At the party, we said goodbye to a few close friends and relatives. We visited other friends one by one. It was sad to say goodbye, but we promised to see everyone again in the future. We promised to write, to call, and to send everyone photographs of our new country. We promised not to forget our friends.

8   We expected life to be difficult at first, and we expected to work very hard. It's difficult to get good jobs because we don't speak much English yet. My wife and I are both engineers, but right now I have a simple job as an electrician. My wife isn't working because she's pregnant. I need to find a second job.

9   My parents and my wife's parents are homesick and unhappy. They don't have friends and they don't speak English. The customs, the food, and the ideas of the American people are very different. Our parents can't adjust easily. They're too old, perhaps. Life is easier for my wife and me. Even so, I wonder when I will be working as an engineer again.

Fumihiko Watanabe, International Businessman

Patricia Hall

10   I travel all the time on business, to Europe and to the United States. I don't say goodbye to my business associates because I call them every day during a business trip. In fact, I don't say goodbye to anybody except my wife and kids. They aren't sad because they know that I'll return in a week or ten days. Believe it or not, they're happy when I go on a trip! I promise to bring them presents. I always keep that promise. The longer the trip, the bigger the gifts!

Concluding Thoughts

11   In all three of the examples above, people leave their home countries. They say goodbye to friends and relatives, and make different kinds of promises. For some people, leaving home is a sad experience. For others, it is a happy, exciting experience, to be repeated, they hope, many times in their lives.

Comprehension Questions

Answer the questions orally or in writing.

1. This article discussed ____ .
   a. one kind of person who leaves home
   b. several kinds of people who leave home
   c. It was not about people who leave home.

2. The author believes that saying goodbye is ____ .
   a. always difficult
   b. never difficult
   c. sometimes difficult

3. Each person in the article made some promises to other people. What promises did they make?

The foreign student _____

_____

The emigrant family _____

_____

The international businessman _____

_____

4. Can you think of other promises that foreign students commonly make to their friends and relatives? That emigrants make? Travelers? Businessmen?

_____

_____

5. Which of the three stories did you like the best? Why? Discuss your ideas in class.

6. Why are some people happy when they leave home? Why are some people sad? Which kind of person are you?

EXERCISES AND FURTHER READINGS

A. Reference

Directions: Read the sentences. The underlined pronouns it and they refer to a noun phrase in the first sentence. Write the noun phrase in the blank.

> EXAMPLE: Many students study in foreign countries. Often they need to learn a new language.
>
> THEY = *students (who study in foreign countries)*

1. Some students have goodbye parties. They say goodbye to friends and relatives at these parties.

   THEY = _____

2. There is always food at goodbye parties. It is usually the departing student's favorite dish.

   IT = _____

3. Students and businessmen need money when they travel. Many parents and employers send it every month.

   THEY = _____

   IT = _____

4. When their children leave home, mothers always cry because they feel worried and sad.

   THEY = _____

5. Friends and relatives promise to write. They also promise to take care of everything at home.

   THEY = _____

6. The last goodbye is at the airport. It is the most difficult goodbye of all.

   IT = _____

7. Watanabe, a businessman, travels to Europe on business regularly. <u>He</u> goes <u>there</u> at least three times a year.

HE = _____

THERE = _____

B. Order

Directions: Read the list of activities of a traveling student. The list is not in order. What does a student usually do first (1st), second (2nd), third (3rd), etc.? Put a number next to each activity to show your idea about the best order. Do your classmates agree with you?

EXAMPLE: _1_ Take the TOEFL test.

_3_ Take the TOEFL again.

_4_ Enter an American university.

_2_ Study English.

____ Go to the airport.

____ Buy a plane ticket.

____ Say goodbye to friends.

____ Pack a suitcase.

____ Say goodbye to parents.

C. Read: A Farewell Party

BEFORE YOU BEGIN: What does the word *farewell* mean? Ask your classmates or your teacher.

Note: you will need to guess what kind of reading article this might be and who it might be about.

President Throws Party for Departing King

Last night the President gave a farewell party for the King, who is leaving for his country today. The King and his family visited this country for two weeks. The trip was a pleasure trip, not a business trip.

The goodbye dinner included the King's favorite food as well as some traditional dishes from this country. After dinner, singers and dancers entertained the King and his family. Then the President and the King exchanged gifts. Photographers and reporters recorded the events.

The King said to reporters, "I am happy to be in this country and to meet so many friendly people. My wife and my children feel sad to leave. We promise to visit again and to invite your President to visit us very soon."

Now answer these questions orally or in writing. Work with one or two classmates. Note: GUESS. The answers are not stated directly in the article. You need to make inferences (see Chapter 1 for explanation and examples), and you need to imagine your own details.

1. What kind of article do you think this is? ____
   a. an article from a book
   b. a newspaper article
   c. a letter
   How do you know?

2. Who are the people in the article? What countries could they be from?

3. Why is the King visiting the President's country?

4. Why is the President giving the King and his family a dinner party?

5. Who do you think came to the party?

6. Why did the reporters and photographers go to the farewell party?

D. Read: A Message

```
                    WESTERN UNION
Dennis Weisbrod

Bussum, Holland

ARRIVED  SAFELY  AT  SCHOOL  STOP  LONG
TRIP  STOP  MISS  YOU  ALREADY  STOP  WILL
WRITE  SOON  STOP  KISSES  STOP  ELLA
```

Answer the questions orally or in writing.

1. What do you think this is?

2. This message is not written in complete sentences. Can you rewrite* it in complete sentences?

3. Who is Ella? Who is Dennis? (Make a guess.)

4. Why is Ella writing Dennis this message? Can you describe their situation? (Make a guess.)

E. Read: Promises, Promises

Directions: Read the story. It is not finished. After paragraph 5, there are three different endings. Read all three endings. Choose one.

BEFORE YOU BEGIN: An investor is a person who puts money into a business in order to make more money.

Promises, Promises

1   Bob Barkley was an investor. A young, greedy[1] investor. He wanted to get rich fast. He had a plan. First he opened a small office. Then he invited all of his friends and relatives to an office party. Well, not *all* of his friends and relatives—just his *rich* friends and relatives. He had food, music, and drinks.

---

*to rewrite (v) = to write again

[1]greedy (adj) = wanting more than you need

2   When everybody was feeling good, he stopped the music. He said to his rich friends and relatives, "I have a plan. This plan will make all of you rich. Give me at least $5000, and I promise to double² your money in one year."

3   Everybody was surprised, but interested. Bob talked to his friends and relatives for an hour. He explained his plan in detail. He made a lot of promises. Most importantly, he promised to double everyone's investment. Eventually, the party ended. Everybody agreed³ to send Bob their money. The friends and relatives went home smiling and happy, thinking about getting rich. But one uncle was thinking carefully.

4   The next week, Bob received a total of $50,000 from his friends and relatives. He bought a plane ticket and left for South America. "I can invest the money later," he thought to himself. When he arrived in Rio de Janeiro, he checked into a beautiful, expensive hotel.

5   But Bob's uncle was very smart and very rich. He was also a judge. After the office party, he gave Bob $15,000, not because he wanted to double his money, but because he wanted to test Bob. Needless to say, Bob failed the test. After Bob disappeared, the uncle asked a lot of questions and learned that Bob was in Brazil.

Now choose an ending for this story.

Ending #1:

Six months later, Bob returned from South America with only $300 in his pocket. His uncle, the judge, and the police were waiting for him at the airport. The uncle made Bob a promise: "I promise to give you a place to live, for free, for the next ten years—the city jail."

Ending #2:

Bob's uncle called all of the friends and relatives together for a meeting. He said, "I'm going to South America to look for Bob. I promise to bring him back and to return your money to all of you." Everybody agreed. The uncle left the next day. A month passed, then several more months. The uncle didn't write and he didn't call. A year passed, then another year. Today, the friends and relatives are still waiting.

Ending #3

In South America, Bob tried to enjoy himself, but it was difficult. He spent money for one week, but he wasn't happy. He thought about his friends and relatives and about the promises he had made them. He thought about his uncle the judge. His uncle was

---

²to double (v) = to increase by two times

³to agree (v) = to have the same idea as another person; to consent

smart, and probably knew everything. Bob called him from Brazil. He promised his uncle to fly home the next day and to return the money to his friends and relatives.

Note: If you don't like *any* of the endings, write your own ending here:

_____

_____

_____

_____

_____

When you are finished, discuss the different endings with your classmates.

THE WORD SECTION

A. Selective Reading: Cross Out Unrelated Word

Directions: Cross out the word that does not belong in the group. (When you finish, try to explain your answers to your classmates.)

EXAMPLE: books   pencils   ~~food~~   pens   paper

EXPLANATION: Books, pencils, pens, and paper are school supplies. Food does not belong in this group.

1. studying   talking   eating   drinking   listening to music   dancing

2. mother   father   friend   brother   sister   cousin   uncle

3. happy   promise   sad   worried   excited   nervous

4. relatives   friends   family   parties   parents

5. airport   train station   bus station   school   taxi stand

B. Analogies

Directions: Complete the analogies by choosing one of the four words. Write the word in the blank. If you do not remember what an analogy is, review the explanation in Chapter 1 and study the following examples carefully.

EXAMPLE 1: television : watch (*v*)   book : *read*
               school   read   title   information

EXAMPLE 2: Monday : *day*   October : month
               week   November   date   day

Notice: The relation between each pair of words is equal.

1. name : person   _____ : book
title   read   student   chapter

2. take : photograph   _____ : letter
paper   write   send   airmail

3. husband : _____   aunt : uncle
son   daughter   mother   wife

4. arrive : say hello   leave : _____
say "I'm fine"   say goodbye   cry   say "how are you?"

5. _____ : male   sister : female
boy   man   brother   uncle

6. cry : sad   laugh : _____
happy   worried   party   fun

C. Antonyms

Antonyms are words that have opposite meanings. The antonym of *hot* is *cold,* because the words *hot* and *cold* have opposite meanings. What is the antonym of *right?* Did you guess *left?* Your guess is correct. But *right* has another meaning; it also means *correct.* In the last sentence, we can say: Your guess is right. Therefore, another antonym of the word *right* is *wrong.* Learning antonyms can help you build your vocabulary in English.

Directions: Fill in the blanks with an antonym of each word. Note: More than one answer might be appropriate.

EXAMPLE: hello   *goodbye* _____

1. new _____

2. father _____

3. early _____

4. night _____

5. happy _____

6. man _____

7. come _____

8. difficult _____

9. no one _____

10. poor _____

11. same _____

12. bigger _____

D. Word Forms: Prefix *un-*

In the last exercise, perhaps you wrote *unhappy* as an antonym for *happy*. This is correct (*sad* is also right), because *un-* means *not*. *Unhappy* means "not happy."

Un- is a prefix. It is not a complete word. It is attached to the beginning of a complete word (*pre-* means "before" or "in front of"). However, *un-* cannot be attached to all words. Of course, your dictionary can help you learn which words can be used with *un-,* but other people can help you, too.

Directions: Ask a native speaker of English to tell you some words that being with *un-*. If necessary, ask about the spelling: "How do you spell that word?" Write down each word in your book or on a piece of paper. Bring your list of words to class.

List of words beginning with un-

_____   _____

_____   _____

_____   _____

CHAPTER 3

Travel

PREREADING ACTIVITIES

Part 1: Travel Problems

Chapter 3 is about travel. The first part of the reading article in this chapter discusses problems that students have when they travel. You have probably traveled several times. Did you have any problems?

A.   Look at the list of travelers' problems below. If you have had the same problem, write YES on the line next to the problem. If you did not have the same problem, write NO. If you can think of a different problem, complete sentence number 8.

*Have you had
this problem?*

1. Sometimes travelers lose their suitcases.   _____

2. Sometimes airlines (buslines, trains, etc.) lose travelers' suitcases.   _____

3. Sometimes travelers forget their suitcases.   _____

4. Sometimes travelers lose their tickets.   _____

5. Sometimes travelers forget their tickets.   _____

6. Sometimes travelers miss their planes (buses, trains, etc.).   _____

7. Sometimes travelers get on the wrong plane (bus, train, etc.).   _____

8. Sometimes travelers forget to put something important in their suitcases.   _____

9. Sometimes travelers _____

   _____   _____

B.   Next, sit with two or three classmates. As a group, choose one (or more) of the problems from the list above. Answer the following three questions about this problem (number ____):

1. Do you think that this is a serious problem?
   Yes ☐   No ☐

2. How do travelers probably feel when they have this problem?
   Not worried ☐   A little worried ☐   Very worried ☐

3. What should travelers do if they have this problem?
   a. Ask a stranger for help ☐   **c.** Call a friend ☐
   b. Call relatives ☐   **d.** (Other) _____

C.   Has anyone in your group (class) had any of the travel problems on the list? If so, ask him or her these questions:

1. Were you alone when you had this problem?
   Yes ☐   No ☐

2. How did you feel when you had this problem?

Not worried ☐   A little worried ☐   Very worried ☐

3. What did you do when you had this problem?
   a. Asked a stranger for help   **c.** Called a friend
   b. Called relatives   **d.** Other (describe) _____

   _____

4. Did you solve this problem?

Yes, right away ☐   Yes, but much later ☐   No ☐

If several classmates have had travel problems, discuss their answers to the four questions above. Were their problems similar or different? Were their feelings similar or different? Were their solutions similar or different?

Part 2: Advice for Travelers

The second part of the reading article in Chapter 3 discusses advice for travelers. If you do not know the word *advice,* look it up in your dictionary. Which of the following words is similar to the word *advice?* Circle the similar word. Cross out the words with a different meaning:

ADVICE = problem   suggestion   feeling   solution

Now think of your own travels. Who gave you advice before you left home? (Check one or more.)

1. my mother ____

2. my father ____

3. my friends ____

4. my wife/husband ____

5. my children ____

6. my employer ____

7. my co-workers (people who work in your company) ____

8. (other) _____

Think about the advice that these people gave you. Was it good advice? Did you and your classmates receive advice from similar kinds of people? Different kinds of people?

Now imagine that you are giving travel advice to some students who have not traveled before. What travel advice can you give them? Look at the two examples:

EXAMPLE 1: Take one suitcase. (Grammar structure = imperative)

EXAMPLE 2: You should take one suitcase. (Grammar structure = *should* + verb)

Your advice to students who have not traveled before:

1. _____

2. _____

3. _____

Discuss your advice with your classmates. Do you and your classmates have similar advice for travelers? Different advice? Be prepared to compare your advice with the advice in the reading article.

Part 3: Survey and Predict

Read the list of key words. Then look at the reading article that begins on page 52. Read the title and the headings, and look at the illustration. They give you an idea about the topics in the article. Check the topics that will probably be in this article.

_____ reasons for traveling

_____ saying goodbye to family and friends

_____ learning English

_____ buying airplane tickets

_____ getting on the wrong plane

_____ travel problems

_____ studying in a new school

_____ a story about one person's travel problems

Key Words

problem	**to lose**	**airplane, plane**
reason	**to forget**	**advice**
to travel	**ticket**	**interesting**
traveler	**suitcase**	**story**

Warm-up Selective Reading: Circle Same Words

Directions: Circle all the words that are the same as the word on the left.

1. cities: city   cited   cities   cities   sits   sifts

2. reason: reason   raisin   reason   season   reason

3. different: difficult   different   indifferent   diligent

4. traveler: traveler   travel   traveling   frivolous

5. plane: plan   plane   blame   prone   flame   plane

6. lose: lose   loss   lose   loose   hose   toes   lose

7. ticket: thicket   ticker   ticket   fickle   ticket

8. one: ore   one   won   on   one   are   one   own

READING ARTICLE: Travel

A.   TRAVEL By Paragraph

1   In the past, many people never left their home towns. Nowadays, more and more people travel to other cities or to other countries. Some people travel to visit friends and relatives. Other people travel to see beautiful or famous places. Businessmen travel because of their work. In other words, people travel for many different reasons.

FROM THE ARTICLE: The main idea in paragraph 1 is ___ .
  a. In the past, people never traveled
  b. Most people travel because of business
  c. People travel for a lot of reasons

FROM YOUR KNOWLEDGE: Paragraph 1 lists three different reasons for traveling. Can you think of other reasons for traveling? Write your ideas here:

_____

_____

2   Many students are also travelers. They leave their homes and travel to a school in a different city or country. Sometimes these student travelers have problems. In the next paragraph, one student describes a travel problem that he experienced.

FROM THE ARTICLE: Paragraph 2 was about ___ .
  a. one student's problem
  b. student travelers
  c. leaving home

THINK AHEAD: Read the last sentence in paragraph 2 again. Paragraph 3 will probably be about ___ .
  a. one student
  b. businessmen
  c. reasons for traveling

Takashi's Story

3   Hello. My name is Takashi. My home is in Tokyo, Japan. A few years ago, I went to California in order to study English. When my plane landed in Los Angeles, I was really excited. At last I was in California! I needed to take another plane from Los Angeles to my school in another California city. The airport was confusing, but I finally got on a plane. I ate a snack, read a boring magazine, and fell asleep. When I woke up, the plane was starting to land. I looked out the window. I knew that my school was near the ocean, but I couldn't see any water. I asked the flight attendant, "Where is the ocean?"

He answered, "The ocean is more than a hundred miles from here."

"Oh, no!" I thought. "Where am I?"

I finally had to take *another* plane to my school. I'll never forget that trip!

FROM THE ARTICLE: Why couldn't Takashi see the ocean from the plane window? Check one.

     a. _____ The ocean was far away.

     b. _____ Takashi was on the wrong plane.

     c. _____ Both *a* and *b* are correct.

FROM YOUR KNOWLEDGE: What are some other travel problems that you or your classmates have had? Talk about one problem in class or write it here:

_____

_____

_____

---

4   Takashi got on the wrong plane. Other students may have different problems when they travel. For instance,[1] they may lose their airplane ticket or forget their suitcases. Sometimes the airlines lose their suitcases. When this happens, the student and his or her suitcase might go to different countries. Problems such as these can be very difficult for students. How can they avoid[2] problems when they travel?

---

[1]for instance (expr) = for example

[2]to avoid (v) = to stay away from

FROM THE ARTICLE: The word *this* is used in paragraph 4 (When this happens, ...).

THIS = _____

THINK AHEAD: Paragraph 5 will probably discuss ____ .
   a. Takashi's problem
   b. different reasons for traveling
   c. advice for students who travel

5   Students can often give each other helpful advice about traveling to other countries. Here are some examples of their advice. The examples were collected by a teacher of ESL (English as a Second Language):

1. Make airplane reservations early.
2. Take only one big suitcase.
3. Buy a ticket at a discount.[3]
4. Ask friends to take you to the airport.
5. Remember your gate number at the airport.
6. Learn how to pronounce the name of the city where you are going.

Most of the students gave similar advice. Maybe most students have similar problems when they travel.

FROM THE ARTICLE: Paragraph 5 is about ____.
   a. one teacher's advice about traveling
   b. students' advice about traveling
   c. similar problems that students have

FROM YOUR KNOWLEDGE AND FROM THE ARTICLE: Is your advice to travelers similar to the advice in paragraph 5? Do you have some advice that is different?

My advice is similar ☐   different ☐.

THINK AHEAD: In the next paragraph (6), watch for the words *serious* and *interesting*. What do these words describe?

---

[3]at a discount (expr) = at a cheaper price than normal

6   People travel for different reasons. Some people travel because of business. Others travel to visit relatives or to visit a famous place. Student travelers are a special group. They travel to a new school, and they often travel alone. They sometimes have problems when they travel. At the moment, the problems seem serious. But later, the problems can become interesting stories, like Takashi's story. A travel problem can become an adventure story, and the story can make us laugh.

FROM THE ARTICLE: Paragraph 6, the conclusion of the article, says that travel problems can become interesting stories later. Do you agree?

Yes, I agree. ☐   No, I don't agree. ☐

B. TRAVEL Complete Reading

1   In the past, many people never left their home towns. Nowadays, more and more people travel to other cities or to other countries. Some people travel to visit friends and relatives. Other people travel to see beautiful or famous places. Businessmen travel because of their work. In other words, people travel for many different reasons.

2   Many students are also travelers. They leave their homes and travel to a school in a different city or country. Sometimes these student travelers have problems. In the next paragraph, one student describes a travel problem that he experienced.

Takashi's Story

3   Hello. My name is Takashi. My home is in Tokyo, Japan. A few years ago, I went to California in order to study English. When my plane landed in Los Angeles, I was really excited. At last I was in California! I needed to take another plane from Los Angeles to my school in another California city. The airport was confusing, but I finally got on a plane. I ate a snack, read a boring magazine, and fell asleep. When I woke up, the plane was starting to land. I looked out the window. I knew that my school was near the ocean, but I couldn't see any water. I asked the flight attendant, "Where is the ocean?"

He answered, "The ocean is more than a hundred miles from here."

"Oh, no!" I thought. "Where am I?"

I finally had to take *another* plane to my school. I'll never forget that trip!

4   Takashi got on the wrong plane. Other students may have different problems when they travel. For instance, they may lose their airplane ticket or forget their suitcases. Sometimes the airlines lose their suitcases. When this happens, the student and his or her suitcase might go to different countries. Problems such as these can be very difficult for students. How can they *avoid* problems when they travel?

5   Students can often give each other helpful advice about traveling to other countries. Here are some examples of their advice. The examples were collected by a teacher of ESL (English as a Second Language):

1. Make airplane reservations early.
2. Take only one big suitcase.
3. Buy a ticket at a discount.
4. Ask friends to take you to the airport.
5. Remember your gate number at the airport.
6. Learn how to pronounce the name of the city where you are going.

Most of the students gave similar advice. Maybe most students have similar problems when they travel.

6   People travel for different reasons. Some people travel because of business. Others travel to visit relatives or to visit a famous place. Student travelers are a special group. They travel to a new school, and they often travel alone. They sometimes have problems when they travel. At the moment, the problems seem serious. But later, the problems can become interesting stories, like Takashi's story. A travel problem can become an adventure story, and the story can make us laugh.

Comprehension Questions

Answer the questions orally or in writing.

1. This article discussed ____ .
   a. reasons why students travel
   b. problems when students travel
   c. both *a* and *b*

2. According to this article, students ____ .
   a. usually make airplane reservations early
   b. sometimes have travel problems
   c. travel for different reasons

3. The author of this article believes that travelers can tell interesting stories about travel problems.

   T   F

4. "Take only one big suitcase." This is an example of ____ .
   a. advice
   b. a problem
   c. one student's problem

5. Think about Takashi's problem. Who probably made the mistake—Takashi or someone at the airport? Try to explain your answer.

EXERCISES AND FURTHER READINGS

A. Reference

Directions: Read the sentences. There are pronouns (*it, they, them, he, one,* etc.) and an adverbial (*there*) underlined in some sentences. Each underlined word refers to a noun phrase that came before the underlined word. Write the noun phrase in the blank.

> EXAMPLE: Traveling by plane is fast. However, <u>it</u> is also expensive.
>
> IT = *traveling by plane*

1. Students sometimes have problems when <u>they</u> travel.

   THEY = _____

2. Tourists usually want to see beautiful places. Often, <u>they</u> must travel long distances to see <u>them</u>.

   THEY = _____

   THEM = _____

3. Some students go to schools in a different country. Their relatives give <u>them</u> advice before <u>they</u> leave.

   THEM = _____

   THEY = _____

4. A teacher asked her students to give advice about traveling. They wrote it on a piece of paper. She collected all the papers and returned them the next day with comments.

> THEY = _____
>
> IT = _____
>
> SHE = _____
>
> THEM = _____

5. People often have similar problems when they travel. However, they sometimes solve them in different ways.

> THEY = _____
>
> THEY = _____
>
> THEM = _____

6. Takashi took a plane to Santa Barbara. But he arrived there late because he got on the wrong one at first, and it took him to a different city.

> HE = _____
>
> THERE = _____
>
> HE = _____
>
> ONE = _____
>
> IT = _____
>
> HIM = _____

B. Order

Directions: Read the list of events from Takashi's story (paragraph 3). The list is not in the right order, according to the story. Put a number next to each event to show the correct order. Try to remember the order. Try not to look back at the story.

_____ fell asleep

_____ talked to the flight attendant

_____ took another flight

_____ read a magazine

_____ got on the plane

_____ looked out of the airplane window

C. Fact or Opinion

Directions: Read the statements. If the statement is a fact, circle **F.** If the statement is someone's opinion, circle **O.**

		Fact	Opinion
EXAMPLE:	An airplane has wings.	(F)	O
	Traveling by plane is fun.	F	(O)

	Fact	*Opinion*
1. Students give the best travel advice.	F	O
2. People travel for different reasons.	F	O
3. Many people travel to see beautiful places.	F	O
4. Students should leave their home town to go to college.	F	O
5. People who travel by plane have more problems than people who travel by train.	F	O

D. Grammatical Word Groups: Identify

Directions: Read the group of words in parentheses. Then read the groups that follow. Underline all of the examples of the same kind of group (= groups that have the same grammatical structure). (See Chapter 1, the section on Grammatical Word Groups, for more explanation and examples.) Remember: In this exercise, pay attention to form, not to meaning.

EXAMPLE: (large airplane)   <u>long train</u>   the taxi   take a bus   <u>beautiful car</u>
give advice   <u>old suitcase</u>

EXPLANATION: *Large airplane* is a grammatical group that consists of an adjective *(large)* and a noun *(airplane)*. The underlined groups (long train, beautiful car, old suitcase) also consist of an adjective and a noun.

1. (take a bus)   a long bus trip   lose a suitcase   forget the ticket   feel worried   give some advice

2. (an interesting trip)   the wrong gate   the helpful flight attendant   the traveler left   a sad story   a trip to Europe

3. (in my pocket)   put on my jacket   lose your ticket   on the plane   in your suitcase   under the seat   avoid problems

4. (give advice)   difficult problems   see the ocean   far from home   understand the instructions   make suggestions   travel frequently

5. (land in Los Angeles)   drive to New York   arrive at school   study English beautiful California   travel to Europe

E. Grammatical Word Groups: Read

Directions: The paragraph below (1) is divided vertically into grammatical word groups. Read it as quickly as you can. Then read the same paragraph divided horizontally (2). Finally, read the paragraph with normal spacing (3).

1. Vertical

Now and then,
travelers get separated
from their suitcases.
For example,
airline travelers
sometimes arrive
at their destination
and discover
that their suitcases
went to another city.
The airline
is responsible for your suitcases
in this case.
The airline must try
to find your suitcases quickly,
and deliver them
to your home or hotel.
If the airline
cannot find your luggage,
it must pay you
for your loss.

2. Horizontal

   Now and then,   travelers get separated   from their suitcases.   For   example,   airline travelers   sometimes arrive   at their destination   and discover   that

their suitcases   went to another city.   The airline   is responsible for your suitcases   in this case.   The airline must try   to find your suitcases quickly,   and
deliver them   to your home or hotel.   If the airline   cannot find your luggage,   it
must pay you   for your loss.

3. Normal Spacing

Now and then, travelers get separated from their suitcases. For example, airline
travelers sometimes arrive at their destination and discover that their suitcases went to
another city. The airline is responsible for your suitcases in this case. The airline must
try to find your suitcases quickly, and deliver them to your home or hotel. If the airline
cannot find your luggage, it must pay you for your loss.

F. Read: The Cruise

Cruise-lovers Special!

Cruise the beautiful Caribbean for 10 days on a luxury ocean liner. Featuring: comfortable
rooms—all the food you can eat—exercise facilities and classes—two swimming pools—
music and dancing nightly. Five stops in famous Caribbean ports for shopping, beaches,
restaurants, and night clubs. Student and group discount—15%*!!! Make your reservations today.
    (*Applies only to groups of 20 or more. Must be paid in full at time of reservation.
    No refunds.)

Answer the questions orally or in writing.

1. This is probably _____ .
    a. a newspaper article about traveling
    b. an advertisement in a travel brochure
    c. a paragraph in a book about the Caribbean

2. What do you think a cruise is?

3. If you go on this cruise, what activities can you do?

4. What is your opinion about the 15% discount? Is it a good idea?

5. Have you ever been on a cruise? If so, describe it to the class.

G.   Read: The Olympics

Prereading

The Olympic Games are a popular sporting event. Many people travel to the Olympics from all over the world. How much do you know about the Olympics? Read the list of words below. If the word or phrase is related to the Olympics, check YES. If the word or phrase is not related, check NO.

1.	swimming	YES ☐	NO ☐
2.	four years	YES ☐	NO ☐
3.	nations	YES ☐	NO ☐
4.	bowling	YES ☐	NO ☐
5.	flags	YES ☐	NO ☐
6.	Greece	YES ☐	NO ☐
7.	professional	YES ☐	NO ☐
8.	car racing	YES ☐	NO ☐
9.	horseback riding	YES ☐	NO ☐
10.	painting	YES ☐	NO ☐
11.	national song	YES ☐	NO ☐
12.	domestic	YES ☐	NO ☐
13.	international	YES ☐	NO ☐

Discuss your answers with your classmates. Explain your answers. Before you begin the reading, look up the word *injured* in your dictionary. *Injured* and *hurt* have similar meanings.

The Olympics: Travel Stories

1   1968: Mexico City. 1972: Munich. 1980: Moscow. 1984: Los Angeles. 1988: Seoul. The Olympic Games come once every four years. Many nations send their athletes to the Olympics to compete in different sports. Many of these athletes travel long distances to the Olympics. Sometimes they have problems when they travel. Here is one story about a travel problem that happened many years ago.

2   In 1906, the Olympic Games were in Athens, Greece. Some American athletes were traveling to Athens by ship. This ship was named the S.S Barbarossa. On the way to Athens, the S.S. Barbarossa ran into a big storm. The storm caused huge[1] waves and swells in the ocean. The ship went up and down like a ball. The passengers on the ship fell into the walls and furniture. Some of the passengers were injured, including some American athletes.

3   One of the American athletes on the ship was a runner. He was an excellent runner, and everyone believed that he was going to win his race. However, he lost his race because he had been hurt on the ship. Travel problems ended his Olympic dreams.

4   Another story about Olympic travel problems had a happier ending. In 1948, the Olympics were in St. Moritz, Switzerland. Just before the Games started, people in the United States heard a surprising radio broadcast[2]. The broadcast said that the American Olympic team had spent all of its money while traveling to Switzerland. It didn't have any more money, and therefore could not make the final trip to St. Moritz. Radio and newspaper reporters found the team and asked the team members what had happened to all of their money.

5   The American Olympic team was very surprised to learn this news about their money problems. In fact, they had plenty of[3] money. Where did the story about their money problem come from? Nobody knows. The team told the reporters that the story was false, then the athletes left for St. Moritz. People in the United States were happy to hear this good news, but the reporters were probably disappointed. They had to look somewhere else for a good story.

Answer the questions orally or in writing.

1. In paragraph 1, there is some general information about the Olympics. What did this paragraph tell you about the Olympics? (Write your answer or discuss it with a classmate.)

2. How many stories does this article tell? ____ .

---

[1]huge (adj) = very big

[2]broadcast (n, C) = a radio or television report (v = to broadcast)

[3]plenty of (expr) = a lot of

3. True or false? Some American athletes were injured in Athens.

      T   F

4. This short reading article is mainly ____ .
  a. a comparison of several Olympics
  b. a general description of the Olympics
  c. travel stories related to the Olympics

5. What is one important idea from this article? ____
  a. The United States did not attend the Moscow Olympics.
  b. Many people, including a famous American runner, were hurt while traveling to the 1906 Olympics.
  c. The Olympics are reported on the radio, in the newspaper, and on television.

6. True or false? The Americans who traveled to Switzerland for the 1948 Olympics did not have any money when they arrived in St. Moritz.

      T   F

7. Read the last sentence of the article. Why do you think the reporters were probably disappointed to hear that the American athletes did not have a money problem?

8. Which kind of news do you find more interesting—good news or bad news?

THE WORD SECTION

A. Selective Reading: Cross Out Unrelated Word

Directions: Cross out the word that does not belong in the group. Check the category of the group.

1. airplane   ship   bus   ticket   car   bicycle

    CATEGORY: ____ transportation

                 ____ tourists

                 ____ travel problems

2. teacher   counselor   student   crowd   traveler

    CATEGORY: ____ group of people

                 ____ individual person

                 ____ young person

3. quickly   safely   happy   sadly   slowly

   CATEGORY: ____ adjectives

   ____ adverbs

   ____ nouns

4. study   write   read   fly   listen   talk

   CATEGORY: ____ tourist activities

   ____ animal activities

   ____ student activities

5. money   suitcase   ticket   passport   chair

   CATEGORY: ____ luggage

   ____ kinds of furniture

   ____ things that a traveler needs

B. Analogies

An analogy in the reading about the Olympics describes the movement of a ship in a storm:

   The ship went up and down **like a ball.**

Directions: Answer the questions.

1. Do you think that the analogy of the ship and the ball is useful? Why or why not?

2. Think about a ship in a storm. Match the phrases in column A with an analogy in column B. Choose any analogy that expresses your feelings. Write your own analogy if you wish.

A	*B*	
The movement of the water is like	thunder	boiling mud
_____	an earthquake	an explosion
The sound of the storm is like	a rocking chair	a dancer
_____	a toy	a crash
The ship moves like	a roller coaster	clouds in a storm
_____		

C. Word Association

Look at the word *home*. What is the first word you think of when you see this word?

Write your word here: _____ What words did your classmates write?

     Many words are possible. Some people think of *family* when they see the word *home*. Other people think of their home countries. Still other people think of the houses they live in. As you can see, many answers are correct to a word association question. Your answer is correct for you. Your classmates' answers are correct for them.

Directions: In this exercise, you need to talk to three native speakers of English. Look at the list of stimulus words. One by one, ask each native speaker:

"What is the first word that you think of when you hear the word _____ ?" Write the words under the appropriate column (Speaker 1, Speaker 2, or Speaker 3). If you do not understand a word, ask "How do you spell that word?" Bring your lists to class when you are finished.

STIMULUS WORDS	Speaker 1	Speaker 2	Speaker 3
1. travel			
2. advice			
3. airport			
4. home			
5. beautiful			
6. student			
7. ocean			

1. Which stimulus words caused native speakers to think of the same word? What word did they think of?

2. Which stimulus words caused native speakers to think of different words? What are some of the different words?

3. Are you surprised by any of your results? Are your word associations with the stimulus words similar to those of the native speakers? Different?

CHAPTER 4

What's New?

PREREADING ACTIVITIES

Part 1: Introduction to a Cross-cultural Survey

Read this information together in class.

When you travel to a new country, you need to make several adjustments* to your new environment because some things may be unfamiliar to you. For example, the food is probably different from the food in your home country. Maybe you don't like it at first. Of course, the money is different. You need to "translate" the value of money from dif-

---

*adjustments (n, C, pl) = changes and adaptations that we make in order to fit a new situation

ferent countries into familiar values. This translation takes time, and sometimes it is difficult to figure out quickly. For example, foreigners in the United States have special problems counting change quickly, because most American coins do not have numbers on them. Foreign visitors need to memorize the values and *then* translate. These are just two examples of cultural differences. You might discover that many other things are different, too.

Americans also experience these differences when they travel outside the United States. They, too, need to adjust to different ways of living. This prereading activity asks you to talk to some Americans who have traveled outside the United States, and to find out what cultural differences they have experienced. The activity will be in the form of a survey. First, do Part 2.

Part 2: Vocabulary Activity

Look at the pictures. They represent possible differences among countries. With several other students, make a list of vocabulary from each picture. Any words that your group can think of are okay.

_____

_____

_____

_____

_____

_____

_____

_____

_____

_____

_____

_____

_____

_____

_____

When all the groups are finished, compare the vocabulary in class.

Part 3: Native Speaker Survey

In order to complete the survey, you need to talk to an American. Your teacher will help you find an American to talk to if you don't know any. Follow these steps first:

a. Read the survey (below) carefully in class. Review the vocabulary. Review the directions that you will give to the Americans.

b. Practice introductions and other useful phrases with your teacher.

> EXAMPLES: I'm (we're) from _____ 's English class.
> (your teacher's name)

I'm (we're) conducting a survey.

Have you traveled outside the United States?

What countries have you visited?

How do you spell that?

Can you help me (us) with my (our) survey?

It's about differences between the United States and other countries.

Please answer the questions on this form.

Thanks for your help.

c. Conduct the survey (in class or out of class, according to your teacher's directions). USE THE SURVEY FORM IN THE BOOK. Be prepared to discuss the results in class.

SURVEY OF CULTURAL DIFFERENCES
EXPERIENCED BY INTERNATIONAL TRAVELERS

Name of respondent: _____

Home country or state: _____

Directions: Please answer the questions and circle the numbers that best reflect your experiences traveling in other countries. The results will be used in an ESL class to discuss cross-cultural differences.

1. What countries have you visited in the past five years?

_____

2. In your opinion, which of these countries is the most similar to the United States? _____

Which of these countries is the most different from the United States?

_____

3. For the rest of this survey, choose a country (or a group of similar countries) to compare to the United States.

4. Now look at the list of items. In your experience, how different is each item from the same item in the United States? Circle your opinion on a scale of 1 (very different) to 3 (similar). Then add a brief explanation.

Country (ies): _____

	Very Different	Somewhat Different	Similar
a. The food	1	2	3
EXPLANATION: _____			
b. The money	1	2	3
EXPLANATION: _____			
c. The language	1	2	3
EXPLANATION: _____			
d. Public transportation	1	2	3
EXPLANATION: _____			
e. Standing in lines	1	2	3
EXPLANATION: _____			
f. Attitudes about pets	1	2	3
EXPLANATION: _____			
g. Bathrooms and restrooms	1	2	3
EXPLANATION: _____			
h. (add your own item) _____	1	2	3
EXPLANATION: _____			

THANK YOU

Part 4: Discussion of Survey Results

Compare the results of your surveys in class. What do you think of the experiences and opinions of the Americans? Have you had similar experiences in the United States? In another country?

Part 5: Survey and Predict

Think about the prereading activity that you did. Look at the key words. Then look at the reading article beginning on page 73. Read the title and look at the illustrations. Read the first paragraph and the last paragraph (paragraph 7). When you finish, check one of the statements below.

_____ I am very familiar with the ideas in this reading article.

_____ I don't know anything about the ideas in this reading article.

_____ I am a little familiar with the ideas in this reading article.

Key Words

United States	**adjustment**	**pet**
Americans	**different, difference**	**restroom, bathroom**
travel	**to stand in line**	

READING ARTICLE: Americans and Culture Shock

A. AMERICANS AND CULTURE SHOCK By Paragraph

1   Sometimes people say that Americans live on a big island. Canada is to the north and Mexico is to the south, but other countries are far away. Therefore, many Americans never travel outside the United States.

2   The United States is a huge country, nearly 3000 miles across. Yet Americans can travel easily from one state to another without making major[1] adjustments. Much of the food is similar across the United States, the money is the same, and most people speak

---

[1]major (adj) = large and important

the same language (although the dialects and accents might be different). Some Americans who travel to foreign countries for the first time are shocked[2] at the differences that they find.

FROM THE ARTICLE AND FROM YOUR KNOWLEDGE: Do you agree with the idea in the first sentence of paragraph 1—that Americans live on a big island?

Yes, I agree. ☐   No, I don't agree. ☐

What do you think this idea means? _____

_____

THINK AHEAD: The rest of the reading article will probably discuss

_____
   a. the United States
   b. differences between the United States and other countries
   c. food, money, and language in the United States

3   Of course, Americans expect to find some differences between their country and other countries. For example, they expect the food to be different (although they might ask for hamburgers and french fries anyway). They know that the money is different. They expect that the water might be different in some places. But Americans are not prepared for all of the differences. Here are three that might surprise them.

_____

[2]shocked (adj) = very surprised

FROM THE ARTICLE: What three differences between the United States and other countries are mentioned in paragraph 3?

_____

_____

_____

FROM YOUR KNOWLEDGE: Name three differences between the United States and your country that you noticed when you first came here (to the United States). They can be the same items as those in paragraph 3, or they can be different ones.

_____

_____

_____

FROM THE ARTICLE AND THINK AHEAD: The last sentence of paragraph 3 tells you the topic of the rest of the reading: "Here are three that might surprise them." What do these words refer to?

THREE = _____

THEM = _____

4   One difference between the United States and other countries is in how people stand in line. Most Americans don't think about how they stand in line; they assume that everyone stands in line in the same way. People do not stand in line in the same way, of course. In some countries they stand far apart, in other countries they stand close. In some countries they stand quietly, in other countries they push and shove.

FROM YOUR KNOWLEDGE: How do people stand in line in your country?
(You can use words from paragraph 4 or other words.) _____

_____

5   Another difference might shock Americans who travel. In the United States, many Americans have pets.[3] Americans like animals, especially dogs and cats. They take good care of their pets. They give them special pet food and they make special beds for them. If the pets get sick, Americans take them to a veterinarian.[4] In many countries, however, animals do not live in people's houses. They do not get special food or special treatment. They live in the streets and take care of themselves. If they get sick and hungry, they often die. Americans do not understand this attitude toward animals.

FROM YOUR KNOWLEDGE: Do cats and dogs live in people's houses in your country?
        Yes ☐   No ☐

6   A third difference between the United States and other countries is very shocking for Americans who have never traveled. This difference is in restrooms[5] and bathrooms.[6] In some countries, for example, the design of the toilets is not familiar to Americans. In

---

[3]pets (n, C, pl) = domestic animals that live in people's houses (e.g., dogs and cats)

[4]veterinarian (n, C) = an animal doctor

[5]restrooms (n, C, pl) = public washrooms and toilets

[6]bathrooms (n, C, pl) = toilets and bathing facilities in the home

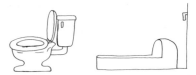

particular, Western and non-Western toilets sometimes look very different. Thus, Americans who travel learn quickly that the Western design is not universal. In addition, Americans are often very upset to discover that, in some countries, public restrooms do not have toilet paper and hand towels. People carry these things with them or they tip[7] a restroom attendant in order to get them. Finally, in private homes, the toilet and bath or shower might be in different rooms. This arrangement is very strange for Americans, because in the United States, the toilet and bath are in the same room.

FROM THE ARTICLE: What three differences between the United States and other countries are discussed in paragraphs 4, 5, and 6?

_____

_____

_____

FROM YOUR KNOWLEDGE: In your travel experience in the United States or in other countries, have you experienced any of the differences that are discussed in paragraphs 4, 5, and 6?

Yes ☐   No ☐

If you answered yes, which of the differences have you experienced?

_____

_____

---

7   These are just a few examples of cultural differences that might shock Americans who travel for the first time. It is good for Americans to travel. By traveling, they can learn how other people live and think. They can learn that customs are not necessarily better or worse in different countries; customs are simply different. Above all[8], Americans can learn that the United States is not an island.

---

[7]to tip (v) = to give a small amount of money to someone (in a restaurant, a restroom, etc.) in exchange for a service

[8]above all (expr) = most importantly

FROM YOUR KNOWLEDGE: Do you believe that Americans are ignorant (not knowledgeable) about other countries and cultures?

Yes, they are ignorant about other cultures. ☐

No, they are not ignorant. They know a lot about other countries and cultures. ☐

What can Americans do in order to become more knowledgeable about other countries and cultures?

_____

_____

_____

B. AMERICANS AND CULTURE SHOCK   Complete Reading

1   Sometimes people say that Americans live on a big island. Canada is to the north and Mexico is to the south, but other countries are far away. Therefore, many Americans never travel outside the United States.

2   The United States is a huge country, nearly 3000 miles across. Yet Americans can travel easily from one state to another without making major adjustments. Much of the food is similar across the United States, the money is the same, and most people speak the same language (although the dialects and accents might be different). Some Americans who travel to foreign countries for the first time are shocked at the differences that they find.

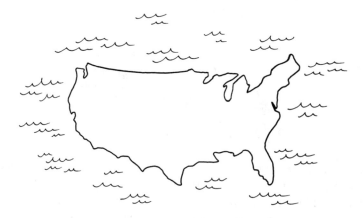

3   Of course, Americans expect to find some differences between their country and other countries. For example, they expect the food to be different (although they might ask for hamburgers and french fries anyway). They know that the money is different. They expect that the water might be different in some places. But Americans are not prepared for all of the differences. Here are three that might surprise them.

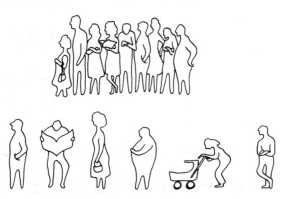

4   One difference between the United States and other countries is in how people stand in line. Most Americans don't think about how they stand in line; they assume that everyone stands in line in the same way. People do not stand in line in the same way, of course. In some countries they stand far apart, in other countries they stand close. In some countries they stand quietly, in other countries they push and shove.

5   Another difference might shock Americans who travel. In the United States, many Americans have pets. Americans like animals, especially dogs and cats. They take good care of their pets. They give them special pet food and they make special beds for them. If the pets get sick, Americans take them to a veterinarian. In many countries, however, animals do not live in people's houses. They do not get special food or special treatment. They live in the streets and take care of themselves. If they get sick and hungry, they often die. Americans do not understand this attitude toward animals.

6   A third difference between the United States and other countries is very shocking for Americans who have never traveled. This difference is in restrooms and bathrooms. In some countries, for example, the design of the toilets is not familiar to Americans. In particular, Western and non-Western toilets sometimes look very different. Thus, Americans who travel learn quickly that the Western design is not universal. In addition, Americans are often very upset to discover that, in some countries, public restrooms do not have toilet paper and hand towels. People carry these things with them or they tip a rest room attendant in order to get them. Finally, in private homes, the toilet and bath or shower might be in different rooms. This arrangement is very strange for Americans, because in the United States, the toilet and bath are in the same room.

7   These are just a few examples of cultural differences that might shock Americans who travel for the first time. It is good for Americans to travel. By traveling, they can learn how other people live and think. They can learn that customs are not necessarily better or worse in different countries; customs are simply different. Above all, Americans can learn that the United States is not an island.

Comprehension Questions

Answer the questions orally, or in writing.

1. This article is written from the viewpoint of ____ .
   a. an American who is traveling in a foreign country
   b. a non-American who is traveling in the United States
   c. an American who is traveling in the United States

2. From the article, we get the idea that ____ .
   a. many Americans do not know very much about other countries because they do not often travel outside the U.S.
   b. Americans do not like foreigners because the customs are different
   c. foreigners do not like Americans because Americans do not know anything about other countries

3. According to the article, how do Americans feel about pets? How do people from your country feel about pets? Talk about your answers in class.

4. This article says that people from different countries stand in lines in different ways. Do you agree? Can you give some examples from your experience? Talk about your ideas in class.

5. Most reading articles on the topic of cultural differences do not talk about bathrooms. How should travelers learn about this subject? Check the statements that match your opinion. Write your own opinion if you wish. Then discuss your ideas in class.

   a.____ The topic of cultural differences in bathrooms should be discussed in books and reading articles.

   b.____ This topic should never be discussed in books and articles.

   c.____ People should learn about different styles of bathrooms from friends and relatives who travel.

   d.____ People should learn about different styles of bathrooms by experience.

   e.____ People should ask travel agents about this topic.

   f. ____ This reading article is a good introduction to the topic of cultural differences in bathrooms.

   g.____ This reading article should not discuss bathrooms.

EXERCISES AND FURTHER READINGS

A.   Reference

Directions: Read the sentences. The underlined words (*it, they, them, others,* etc.) refer to a previous noun phrase. Write the noun phrase in the blank.

   EXAMPLE: New food looks different. <u>It</u> smells different, too.

   IT = *new food*

1. Beef and lamb are my favorite meats. However, I am not familiar with how <u>they</u> are prepared in the United States.

   THEY = _____

2. In most countries, the bills and coins have numbers on <u>them</u>. Therefore, <u>they</u> are easy to understand.

   THEM = _____

   THEY = _____

3. People who travel to other countries need to know how to stand in line. In some countries, <u>they</u> need to stand quietly. In <u>others</u>, <u>they</u> need to push.

  THEY = _____

  OTHERS = _____

  THEY = _____

4. American coins don't have numbers on <u>them</u>. Foreigners look for <u>them</u>, but <u>they</u> can't find <u>them</u>.

  THEM = _____

  THEM = _____

  THEY = _____

  THEM = _____

5. Drinking coffee in class is an accepted classroom custom in some American universities. <u>It</u> is not a custom in many universities in other countries.

  IT = _____

6. Good public restrooms in the United States are supplied with toilet paper, paper towels or electric hand driers, and soap. Americans expect to find <u>these supplies</u> in restrooms in other countries, but sometimes <u>they</u> are shocked to find none of <u>them</u>.

  THESE SUPPLIES = _____

  THEY = _____

  THEM = _____

B. Levels of Generalization

Directions: Read the groups of words or phrases. One word or phrase in the group is GENERAL. The other two words or phrases are SPECIFIC examples of the general word or phrase. Write **G** in front of the general words. Write **S** in front of the specific words.

  EXAMPLE: _S_ aunt

       _S_ cousin

       _G_ relative

1. ____ nickels

  ____ coins

  ____ quarters

2. ____ to interview

____ to ask questions

____ to get answers

3. ____ cat

____ pet

____ dog

4. ____ behavior in lines

____ stand close

____ stand far apart

5. ____ smoke in class

____ chew gum in class

____ customs in class

C. Agree/Disagree

Directions: Read the statements. Do you agree or disagree with them? Discuss your answers in class.

1. Americans are ignorant about other cultures.

I agree. ☐   I don't agree. ☐

2. Public restrooms should have hot water for washing hands.

I agree. ☐   I don't agree. ☐

3. It is difficult to adjust to the food in the United States.

I agree. ☐   I don't agree. ☐

4. Students should call teachers by title and last name.

I agree. ☐   I don't agree. ☐

5. Every country needs veterinarians.

I agree. ☐   I don't agree. ☐

D. Read: Culture Shock: Two Examples

BEFORE YOU BEGIN: People who move to another country have to adjust to a different culture. Some differences between the home culture and the new culture are easy to see—the food, the money, and the weather. Other differences are not so easy to see—the customs of the people and the way of thinking, for example. All of these differences can be a shock[1] to the newcomer.[2] Often he or she experiences this shock for several weeks or even months after arriving in a new country. The phrase "culture shock" is used to describe this feeling of shock. Culture shock can make people feel depressed[3], angry, and tired. The two paragraphs below describe two people's experiences with culture shock. Hsun Hua is a 35-year-old woman from Taiwan. Naomi is a 28-year-old woman from Japan.

Hsun Hua

"I moved to Hong Kong from Taiwan seven years ago. My husband's home is Hong Kong. This move was a terrible culture shock for me. This sounds ridiculous, because I am Chinese, and over 90 percent of the people in Hong Kong are Chinese. Why did I experience culture shock there? First, because of language. The language used in Hong Kong is Cantonese. Cantonese is a kind of Chinese, but it is totally different from the language we use in Taiwan. I couldn't understand anything, believe it or not, so I lost confidence in myself. Also, Hong Kong is a very crowded city. The crowds of people and the tall, crowded buildings caused me a lot of stress. I always felt like a sardine.[4] Besides this, I was away from my parents, my dear sister, and my best friend. I had no relatives at all in Hong Kong. I was absolutely isolated and lonely there for many months."

Answer the questions orally or in writing.

1. Why did Hsun Hua move to Hong Kong?
2. Why did she feel lonely there?
3. How are Hong Kong and Taiwan similar?
4. How are they different?
5. Hsun Hua says that she felt like a sardine in Hong Kong. Have you ever experienced this feeling? When? Where? Why?

---

[1]shock (n, C) = a sudden surprise

[2]newcomer (n, C) = new + come + -er: a person who has just arrived at a new place

[3]depressed (adj) = very unhappy

[4]a sardine (n, C) = a small fish; sardines are packed closely together in cans

```
┌─────────────────────────────┐
│            ꜾꝊ               │
│  WANTED: Roommate           │
│  to share apartment         │
│  male/female OK             │
│  NONSMOKER, no pets         │
│  ½ rent, share utilities    │
│  Call 229-4516  Ask for     │
│                 Cheryl      │
└─────────────────────────────┘
```

Naomi

"I will tell you about my personal experience with culture shock. It was so surprising for me. One day I was looking at the messages on the school bulletin board. One message caught my eye. It said: 'Wanted: Roommate. Male/Female OK. Nonsmoker.' I wondered what it meant. In Japan we don't have the custom of choosing a roommate by advertising in this way. People who live together are good friends or couples. They aren't strangers. But in the United States, students look for a roommate who is a stranger. Some of them don't care about the sex of their roommates—either a man or a woman is OK. I was very surprised to see this system."

Answer the questions orally or in writing.

1. Where was Naomi when this experience happened?
2. What do you think she was doing at the school?
3. Who do you think wrote the message on the bulletin board?
4. Why was Naomi so surprised when she read the message on the bulletin board?
5. The person who wrote the message didn't care if the roommate was a man or a woman. Do you think all American students have similar ideas about roommates?

E. Read: Classroom Customs

Prereading Activity

Every country has rules for behavior in a classroom. In this activity, compare the rules and customs of your English class with classroom rules in your country. Think about university classes or, if you are not familiar with university classes in your country, think about high school classes. Put **Y** for YES, **N** for NO, and **S** for SOMETIMES.

BEHAVIOR / RULE	My Country	This Class
Students call classmates by first name.		
Students call teachers by first name.		
Students call teachers by title and last name.		
Students have co-educational classes (men and women in the same class).		
Students wear formal clothes or uniform to class.		
Students wear informal clothes to class.		
Teachers wear formal clothes.		
Teachers wear informal clothes.		
Students can eat something in class.		
Students can smoke in class.		
Students must raise hand to speak.		
(Other) _____		

Now write the phrase in the blank that best describes classroom behavior in your country, according to your responses:

Classroom behavior in my country is _____ classroom behavior in the United States.

    a. similar to

    b. a little different from

    c. very different from

Discuss your answers with your classmates and teacher. Then read the following article.

Informality in the American Classroom

1   When students from other countries come to the United States, they are sometimes shocked at the informality in American college and university classes. For example, American professors do not dress up[1] and they generally call students by their first names. Students can speak out in class, especially in small classes, where they do not even need to raise their hands. In addition, in many schools, students can drink coffee, tea, juice, or soft drinks during classes.

2   Foreign students can usually get used to[2] these differences easily. However, two examples of American informality are very difficult for some foreign students to understand. First, students sometimes call their teachers by their first names. Instead of calling a teacher Mr. Smith or Professor Johnson, they call them Tom or Barbara. In some countries, it is not possible for students to "first-name" their teachers. Second, American students sometimes criticize[3] the ideas of their teachers. They might also give their teachers suggestions about changing something in the class. In many countries, students cannot openly criticize their teachers or classes.

3   Thus, some foreign students feel shocked, embarrassed, and uncomfortable in American classrooms. They think that American students do not respect their teachers. They think that there are no rules at all in American classrooms. These foreign students must decide how they will behave. They have two choices. One, they can imitate[4] the behavior of the American students. But in this case, they might feel uncomfortable and disrespectful. Two, they can continue to follow the customs from their home countries. But in this case, the American teachers and students might think that the foreign students are too formal or too quiet.

4   What is the solution to this problem? There is no easy answer. However, time will help to solve the problem, because foreign students will become accustomed to the new behavior. Additionally, it might be helpful to talk about problems in class, openly, with the teacher and with other students. Especially in ESL classes, cross-cultural discussions are interesting, valuable, and therapeutic. Finally, it will be helpful if the American teacher talks about rules of behavior in the American classroom. Behavior is *not* completely free and informal. Some rules exist in every classroom!

---

[1]to dress up (v) = to put on and wear formal clothes

[2]to get used to something (v, expr) = to become accustomed to something

[3]to criticize (v) = 1. to evaluate or judge;   2. to find faults, problems, and mistakes

[4]to imitate (v) = to copy

Answer the questions orally or in writing.

1. According to this article, some American classroom customs are easy for foreign students to adjust to, and some classroom customs are very difficult for them to adjust to. Make a list of the classroom customs mentioned in the article.

   a. Customs easy to adjust to: _____

   _____

   _____

   b. Customs difficult to adjust to: _____

   _____

   _____

2. Do you agree or disagree with the ideas in your answer to question number 1?

3. If your ideas are different from the ideas of the author, what classroom customs do you believe are easy to adjust to? What customs do you believe are difficult to adjust to?

4. What is your definition of *informal classroom behavior*? Give examples from your own experience.

5. The author of the article believes that cross-cultural discussions are very useful in ESL classes. Why does she believe this? Do you agree with her?

THE WORD SECTION

A. Selective Reading: Cross Out Unrelated Word

Directions: Read the group of words. Cross out the word that does not belong in the group. When you finish, try to explain your decisions to your classmates.

> EXAMPLE: plants   trees   islands   ~~coins~~   animals

> EXPLANATION: Coins are made by people. The other words describe natural things. Therefore, the word *coins* does not belong in the group.

1. bills   food   coins   money   change
2. language   accent   pronunciation   lines   speech
3. Alaska   New York   Canada   California   Texas
4. survey   change   adapt   adjust   learn
5. bathroom   toilet   restroom   traveler   shower

B. Selective Reading: Circle Category Word

Directions: Read the group of words. Circle the general category word in each group. The other words will be examples of the category.

> EXAMPLE: beef   meat   pork   lamb   chicken
>
> EXPLANATION: Beef, pork, lamb, and chicken are all examples of *meat.*

1. Ms.   Mr.   Dr.   title   Mrs.   Prof.
2. nickel   dime   quarter   coin   penny
3. relative   aunt   mother   brother   cousin
4. United States   Mexico   Japan   Lebanon   country
5. transportation   plane   bicycle   car   bus   train
6. food   bread   meat   vegetable   fruit   rice
7. dog   pet   cat   bird   hamster
8. surprised   shocked   angry   feelings   upset

C. Analogies

Directions: Complete the analogies by choosing a word from the list. Write the word in the blank.

> EXAMPLE: eat : food   read : *book*
> write   book   eyes   pages   student
>
> EXPLANATION: The relationship between *eat* and *food* is the same as the relationship between *read* and *book*. We eat food; we read books. *Eat* is to *food* as *read* is to *book*.

1. money : nickel   food : _____
   bread   eat   delicious   favorite   market

2. Mr. : man   Ms. : _____
   teacher   girl   boy   woman   title

3. see : eye   _____ : tongue
   hear   smell   taste   sound   feel

4. comfortable : uncomfortable _____ : different
   opposite   similar   custom   new   adjustment

5. businessman : office   teacher : _____
   classroom   student   school   professor   desk

6. school : education   _____ : information
   learn   visit   survey   student   adjustment

D. Word Forms: Compound Words

Many English words are made of two words. A word that is made of two words is called a *compound word*. For example, *sea + sick = seasick*. Can you guess the meaning of *seasick*?

Write your guess here: _____

1. *Directions:* Read the list of compound words and the list of definitions. They are not matched. Draw a line from each word to its definition. Write the appropriate compound word next to each definition. The first one is done for you.

restroom	studying that students do at home _____
homesick	writing done with a pen or pencil _____
suitcase	someone who takes money from people's pockets _____
homework	sadness at being far from home _____
handwriting	a machine that can fly in the air _____
toothache	not allowing air to enter or leave _____
airplane	a public toilet _restroom_ _____
pickpocket	a pain in one of the teeth _____
airtight	a case for carrying clothes _____

2. *Directions:* Now try to write your own definitions for the following words:

blackboard _____

notebook _____

wastebasket _____

classroom _____

headache _____

E. Word Association

Often two people know the same word, but their thoughts and associations with the word are very different. Do you make different word associations than native English speakers do? In order to find out, try this activity with an American whose first language is English.

Directions: Look at each word in the list. Write down the first word that you think of when you read each word. Put your word in the first column, under YOUR WORD. Then read each word to a native English speaker. Ask the person to give you the first word he or she thinks of after hearing the word. (You can use a sentence like: "What do you think of when you hear the word _____ ?") Write the native speaker's word in the second column. When you are finished, discuss your results with your classmates.

	Your Word	*Native Speaker's Word*
America	_____	_____
hamburger	_____	_____
dog	_____	_____
restroom	_____	_____
dollar	_____	_____
foreigner	_____	_____
custom	_____	_____

How similar are your words, your classmates' words, and the native speakers' words? How different are they? Do people who have different word associations "see" the world differently?

CHAPTER 5
Photos

PREREADING ACTIVITIES

Part 1: Snapshots

Bring some snapshots to class

(Note: If you do not have any snapshots, sit with a classmate who has some.)

What kinds of snapshots do you have with you for this exercise? (Check as many as you want.)

RELATIVES: ____

    Parents (mother and father)   ____

    Brother(s) and/or sister(s)   ____

    Husband/wife   ____

Child/children   ____

Aunt(s) and uncle(s)   ____

Cousin(s)   ____

(Other) _____   ____

FRIENDS: ____

Classmate(s)   ____

Boyfriend/girlfriend   ____

Friend(s) from work   ____

Neighbor(s)   ____

(Other) _____   ____

PLACES: ____

My city   ____

My house/apartment   ____

Tourist attraction in or
   near my town   ____

Tourist attraction in
   another city/country   ____

(Other) _____   ____

PETS:

Dog   ____

Cat   ____

(Other)   ____

(OTHER): ____

_____   ____

_____   ____

_____   ____

Now sit with two or three classmates. Show them several of your favorite snapshots. (Choose a photo from each category above if possible.) Explain the snapshots to your classmates. Each classmate will ask you one question about your photos. (Continue until all classmates have shared their snapshots.)

Part 2: Occasions

When do you and your family take pictures (on what *occasions*)? Look at the chart. Read the list under the word *occasion*. Check the appropriate boxes to show how often you take pictures at each occasion (never, sometimes, usually, or always).

OCCASION	Never	Sometimes	Usually	Always
Weddings				
Graduations				
Trips				
Holidays				
Birthdays				
Funerals				
(Other) _____				

Compare your chart with the charts of your classmates. Are your charts similar? Different? Are there similarities and differences according to country?

Ask your teacher to fill out the same chart. Discuss the chart in class. Compare your teacher's chart with your chart. Are there similarities and differences?

Part 3: Survey and Predict

Read the list of key words. Then think about the title of the reading article that begins on page 95. Look at the headings and illustrations. Then read the list of topics below. Put a check next to the topics that you think will be important in this article.

_____ How to make money with photography

_____ Historical changes in photography

_____ Why people take pictures

_____ The development of amateur photography

____ Where people keep their photos

____ Why people study photography

____ Advice for photographers

____ How to become a professional photographer

Key Words

photograph/photo	**to take pictures/photos**	**to develop**
professional	**camera**	**easy/difficult to use**
amateur		

READING ARTICLE: The Development of Amateur Photography: A Historical View

A. THE DEVELOPMENT OF AMATEUR PHOTOGRAPHY: A HISTORICAL VIEW By Paragraph

"OK, everybody, look at me! Now, smile. Say 'cheese!'" (click)

1   The "click" of a camera is a sound that you can hear all over the world. Photographs are everywhere—in magazines, newspapers, textbooks, and in frames and photo albums in our homes. Many photos are taken by professional photographers—that is, people who

sell their photos for a living. Most photographers, though, are not professionals. They are amateurs. Amateur photographers take pictures for personal reasons, not for money. There are now millions of amateur photographers in the world. Why has amateur photography become so popular?

FROM THE ARTICLE: True or false? Amateur photographers sell their photos for a living.

    T   F

THINK AHEAD: The rest of this article will probably discuss ____ .
    a. taking photos for a living
    b. how to sell your photos
    c. amateur photography
    d. how to take a good photograph

FROM THE ARTICLE: Which sentence in paragraph 1 gives information about the rest of the article?

____ The first sentence

____ The last sentence

____ No sentence gives this information

Cameras of the 1800's: A Challenge for Amateurs

2   Nowadays, most cameras are very easy to use. In the 1800's, however, photography was much more difficult. In the first place, the cameras were large and heavy. Also, photographers needed to carry glass plates and chemicals with them in addition to their cameras. They used the plates and chemicals to develop their pictures. In those days, photographers had to develop their pictures right after they took them. Some of the chemicals smelled very bad and burned holes in clothing. One chemical, silver nitrate, made the photographer's fingers turn black. Photography was not easy. Therefore, most photographers were professionals. In 1888, though, a new kind of camera changed the world of photography.

FROM THE ARTICLE: Photography was difficult in the 1800's because ____ .
   a. the cameras were not easy to use
   b. chemicals were difficult to find
   c. most photographers were not professionals

THINK AHEAD: The next paragraph will probably discuss ____ .
   a. life in 1888
   b. changes in photography after 1888
   c. professional photography
   d. photographic chemicals

The Simple Camera

3   This new camera was smaller, cheaper, and easier to use than the older cameras. The film was already inside the camera when you bought it. You just turned a key to advance the film, and you were ready to take pictures. After the film was finished, you sent the whole camera, with the film inside, back to the factory. The factory developed

the film and then sent you back your camera and your pictures. The camera even had a new role of film inside. The inventor of this camera named it the "Kodak." He chose this name because it was short, easy to remember, and people all over the world could pronounce it. At last, cameras were easy to use! The number of amateur photographers grew quickly.

FROM THE ARTICLE: The Kodak was easy to use because ___ .
  a. the photographer didn't need to carry chemicals and glass plates
  b. the name was easy to remember and pronounce
  c. the camera was not expensive

THINK AHEAD: The next part of the reading article will probably discuss ___ .
  a. photographers who took photographs for personal reasons
  b. photographers who took photographs for money
  c. the Kodak camera

Early Amateur Photographers

4   One of the new amateur photographers after 1888 was the President of the United States, Grover Cleveland. He once took his Kodak on a fishing trip. He took pictures all day, but unfortunately he forgot to turn the camera key after each shot. Therefore, the film did not advance, with the result that he did not get any photos of that fishing trip.

5   Other early amateur photographers were more successful. A famous painter named Degas took pictures that looked like his paintings (or perhaps he painted pictures that looked like his photographs). Another amateur, Adam Vroman, took pictures of the American Indians. These photographs are important because they show Indians in a very natural way. However, Vroman's photographs are not personal.

FROM THE ARTICLE: Paragraphs 4 and 5 were mostly about ___ .
  a. fishing trips, paintings, and American Indians
  b. famous people from the late 1880's who were also amateur photographers
  c. the problems that amateur photographers had with their cameras in the late 1880's

THINK AHEAD: What will the next paragraph probably discuss? ___
  a. Photographs of family and friends
  b. Photographs that are not personal
  c. We don't know.

Personal Photos

6   Before the invention of the Kodak camera, most photographers took pictures of famous people or events (for example, of Queen Victoria of England or of the Civil War in the U.S.). With the Kodak, though, amateur photographers easily took pictures of their friends and relatives doing ordinary[1] things. Most of these pictures, sometimes called snapshots, were not of professional quality. The quality was not so important, however, because most amateur photographers did not want a perfect picture to sell. They wanted simple pictures of their family and friends.

FROM THE ARTICLE: True or false? Paragraph 6 says that after 1888, most amateur photographers wanted to take pictures of famous people and events.

     T   F

FROM YOUR KNOWLEDGE: Does your family have any family photographs from the late 1800's or early 1900's? If so, who are the people in your old family photographs?

_____

THINK AHEAD: Paragraph 7 is the last paragraph in the article. It will probably discuss ____ .
   a. cameras from the 1800's
   b. professional photographers
   c. modern cameras

Anyone Can Take Pictures

7   Today,[2] thanks to modern technology, amateur photographers can buy amazing new cameras. In some ways, these cameras are the same as the 1888 Kodak: they are small, light,[3] and easy to use. But in other ways, they are completely different. Some of them are like small computers. The camera takes care of focussing and of adjusting the light.[4] The photographer doesn't have to do anything. That's the secret to the success of amateur photography: a camera that anyone can use to take pictures of anything at any time.

---

[1]ordinary (adj) = common, customary, normal

[2]today (adv) = nowadays, in the present time or age

[3]light (adj) = not heavy

[4]light (n, U) = not darkness

FROM THE ARTICLE AND FROM YOUR KNOWLEDGE: Do you agree with this statement? "With a good camera, anyone can take good pictures."

Yes, I agree. ☐   No, I don't agree. ☐

B. THE DEVELOPMENT OF AMATEUR PHOTOGRAPHY: A HISTORICAL VIEW   Complete Reading

"Ok, everybody, look at me! Now, smile. Say 'cheese!' " (click)

1   The "click" of a camera is a sound that you can hear all over the world. Photographs are everywhere—in magazines, newspapers, textbooks, and in frames and photo albums in our homes. Many photos are taken by professional photographers—that is, people who sell their photos for a living. Most photographers, though, are not professionals. They are amateurs. Amateur photographers take pictures for personal reasons, not for money. There are now millions of amateur photographers in the world. Why has amateur photography become so popular?

Cameras of the 1800's: A Challenge for Amateurs

2   Nowadays, most cameras are very easy to use. In the 1800's, however, photography was much more difficult. In the first place, the cameras were large and heavy. Also, photographers needed to carry glass plates and chemicals with them in addition to their

cameras. They used the plates and chemicals to develop their pictures. In those days, photographers had to develop their pictures right after they took them. Some of the chemicals smelled very bad and burned holes in clothing. One chemical, silver nitrate, made the photographers' fingers turn black. Photography was not easy. Therefore, most photographers were professionals. In 1888, though, a new kind of camera changed the world of photography.

The Simple Camera

3   This new camera was smaller, cheaper, and easier to use than the older cameras. The film was already inside the camera when you bought it. You just turned a key to advance the film, and you were ready to take pictures. After the film was finished, you sent the whole camera, with the film inside, back to the factory. The factory developed

Making pictures
2 ½ x 4 ¼ inches

No. 1A
Autographic Kodak, *Special*
1917 Model

EQUIPMEMT

Kodak Range Finder—a practical device that finds the focus for you.

Optimo Shutter speeded to 1/300 of a second as well as seven intervening, adjustable speeds up to one second.

Fast, sharp-cutting anastigmat lens.   Autographic attachment.

And so handsome is the 1A *Special*, so efficient, that it is no surprise to find incorporated in it such up-to-the-minute features as those noted above.

A second-generation Kodak from the early 1900's

the film and then sent you back your camera and your pictures. The camera even had a new roll of film inside. The inventor of this camera named it the "Kodak." He chose this name because it was short, easy to remember, and people all over the world could pronounce it. At last, cameras were easy to use! The number of amateur photographers grew quickly.

Early Amateur Photographers

4   One of the new amateur photographers after 1888 was the President of the United States, Grover Cleveland. He once took his Kodak on a fishing trip. He took pictures all day, but unfortunately he forgot to turn the camera key after each shot. Therefore, the film did not advance, with the result that he did not get any photos of that fishing trip.

5   Other early amateur photographers were more successful. A famous painter named Degas took pictures that looked like his paintings (or perhaps he painted pictures that looked like his photographs). Another amateur, Adam Vroman, took pictures of the American Indians. These photographs are important because they show Indians in a very natural way. However, Vroman's photographs are not personal.

Personal Photos

6   Before the invention of the Kodak camera, most photographers took pictures of famous people or events (for example, of Queen Victoria of England or of the Civil War in the U.S.). With the Kodak, though, amateur photographers easily took pictures of their friends and relatives doing ordinary things. Most of these pictures, sometimes called snapshots, were not of professional quality. The quality was not so important, however, because most amateur photographers did not want a perfect picture to sell. They wanted simple pictures of their family and friends.

Anyone Can Take Pictures

7   Today, thanks to modern technology, amateur photographers can buy amazing new cameras. In some ways, these cameras are the same as the 1888 Kodak: they are small, light, and easy to use. But in other ways, they are completely different. Some of them are like small computers. The camera takes care of focussing and of adjusting the light. The photographer doesn't have to do anything. That's the secret to the success of amateur photography: a camera that anyone can use to take pictures of anything at any time.

Comprehension Questions

Answer the questions orally or in writing.

1. Make a list of words and phrases that describe the cameras and the process of photography before 1888. The words can be from the article and from your knowledge.

_____

_____

_____

2. What is the difference between a professional photographer and an amateur photographer? Try to use your own words.

_____

_____

_____

3. How are cameras today different from the old Kodak camera that was invented in 1888? (Use your knowledge in addition to the information in the reading article.)

_____

_____

_____

EXERCISES AND FURTHER READINGS

A.   Reference

Directions: Read the sentences. A pronoun is underlined in some sentences. The pronoun refers to a noun phrase that came earlier. Write the noun phrase on the line.

EXAMPLE: Students enjoy parties. In the United States, they often have them on Friday nights.

THEY = _students_

THEM = _parties_

1. A photograph can be special. It can bring back memories of people and places.

IT = _____

2. Most photographers aren't professional. They take pictures for personal reasons, not for money.

THEY = _____

3. The early photographers had to develop the pictures right after they took them .

THEY = _____

THEM = _____

4. When people bought the first Kodak camera, the film was already inside <u>it</u> . <u>It</u> advanced by means of a key that <u>they</u> had to turn.

IT = _____

IT = _____

THEY = _____

5. Many years ago, the Kodak factory took the camera with the used film inside <u>it</u> , developed the film, put in new film, then sent <u>the whole thing</u> back to the customer.

IT = _____

THE WHOLE THING = _____

6. Some amateur photographers believe that <u>they</u> need an expensive camera in order to take a good picture. However, <u>others</u> can take beautiful pictures with an inexpensive <u>one</u> .

THEY = _____

OTHERS = _____

ONE = _____

B. Grammatical Word Groups: Identify

Directions: Read the group of words in parentheses. Underline the same kind of word group in the line. There might be more than one group that is the same kind.

EXAMPLE: (the teacher)   to study grammar   <u>a classroom</u>   on the desk
                   read quickly   <u>the textbook</u>

EXPLANATION: The group of words in parentheses, *the teacher,* is a grammatical word group. It consists of an article, *the,* and a noun, *teacher.* Therefore, in this example, you should underline all words groups of the kind ARTICLE + NOUN (*a, an, the* + noun).

1. (their trip)   my snapshots   professional photographer   your family   take a picture   interesting snapshots

2. (in many cultures)   to eat and drink   on the fishing trip   different customs   in the 1800's   a new language

3. (light camera)   take pictures   interesting snapshots   smelly chemicals   tourists   travel   photos of relatives

4. (take a picture)   American Indian   sell a photo   a nice vacation   painters and photographers   develop the film

5. (is a profession)   studying photography   are amateurs   many friends   develop the film   are easy to use   is a camera

6. (nice photos)   famous people   remember to write   in the camera   take some pictures   boring snapshots

C. Grammatical Word Groups: Read

Directions: The paragraph below is from the reading article. Read it three times, as quickly as possible, first in vertical grammatical word groups, next in horizontal groups, and finally with normal spacing.

1.   Vertical

Cameras in the 1800's
were difficult to use.
Because of this,
professional photographers
took pictures
in their studios.
They took these pictures
on glass and metal plates,
and used strong chemicals
to develop them.
These photographs
were black and white.
Color photography
was developed later,
in the 1900's.

2.   Horizontal

Cameras in the 1800's   were difficult to use.   Because of this,   professional photographers   took pictures   in their studios.   They took these pictures   on glass and metal plates,   and used strong chemicals   to develop them.   These photographs   were black and white.   Color photography   was developed later,   in the 1900's

3. Normal Spacing

Cameras in the 1800's were difficult to use. Because of this, professional photographers took pictures in their studios. They took these pictures on glass and metal plates, and used strong chemicals to develop them. These photographs were black and white. Color photography was developed later, in the 1900's.

D. Fact or Opinion

Directions: Read the statements. Use the reading article and your own knowledge to decide if each statement is a fact or an opinion. Discuss your ideas in class.

> EXAMPLE: 1. Some people carry snapshots in their wallets.
>
> Fact ☑   Opinion ☐
>
> EXPLANATION: This statement is a fact—it is true that some people carry snapshots in their wallets.
>
> 2. Snapshots are the best way to remember friends and relatives.
>
> Fact ☐   Opinion ☑
>
> EXPLANATION: This statement is an opinion. Some people believe that snapshots are the best way to remember friends and relatives. Other people remember friends and relatives in other ways.

1. Professional photographers try to sell their photographs.

Fact ☐   Opinion ☐

2. Photographs appear in newspapers and magazines.

Fact ☐   Opinion ☐

3. Newspaper and magazine photographs are interesting.

Fact ☐   Opinion ☐

4. Amateur photographs are boring.

Fact ☐   Opinion ☐

5. Some cameras are very expensive.

Fact ☐   Opinion ☐

6. A Nikon is the best camera.

Fact ☐   Opinion ☐

E. Read: Who Are They?

Directions: Read the descriptions of the people. Then guess who the people are. (Note: We are speaking in general, not about particular individuals.)

EXAMPLE: These people spend a lot of time in classrooms. They carry books, papers, pencils and chalk with them. They usually stand in front of the class and talk to a group of people in the room. They give tests, grades, and advice about studying.

WHO ARE THEY? *teachers*

1. These people sometimes travel for fun. They visit places that are beautiful and interesting. They often carry a camera and maps. They take a lot of pictures and show them to their friends later. They usually stay in hotels.

    WHO ARE THEY? _____

2. These people travel a lot, but they don't travel for fun. They wear a suit and carry a briefcase. There are a lot of papers in the briefcase. Sometimes they carry a small computer with them. They often travel by plane or by train.

    WHO ARE THEY? _____

3. These people have several different kinds of cameras. They take a lot of pictures all the time. They choose the best photographs and make prints of them. They sometimes put their photographs in museums or galleries. They sell the photographs to people and to magazines.

    WHO ARE THEY? _____

4. These people take a lot of photographs. They bring their film to a class every week. They develop the film in the class, and they make prints. A teacher looks at the prints and gives them advice about the prints. Sometimes these people make the prints again. Finally, a teacher gives these people a grade (A, B, C, . . .) on each print.

    WHO ARE THEY? _____

F. Read: The Operating Manual

New cameras usually come with a booklet called an operating manual. The manual explains how to operate the camera, and usually includes pictures, diagrams and written instructions. The operating instructions below explain how to load film into one kind of camera.

Directions: Read the instructions. Then look at the pictures. Match the pictures with the letter for each picture on the line next to the appropriate instruction.

____ **1.** Open camera back.

____ **2.** Drop film cartridge into chamber.

____ **3.** Push film leader onto spool.

____ **4.** Connect perforations with sprocket teeth.

____ **5.** Push film advance lever.

____ **6.** Close camera back.

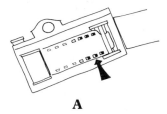

A

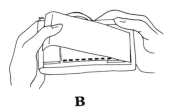

B

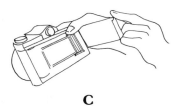

C

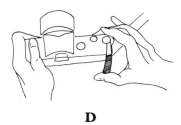

D

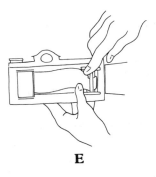

E

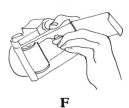

F

G. Read: Where Do You Keep Your Photos?

Answer the questions before you read:

Where do you and your family keep your photos? Check more than one location if necessary.

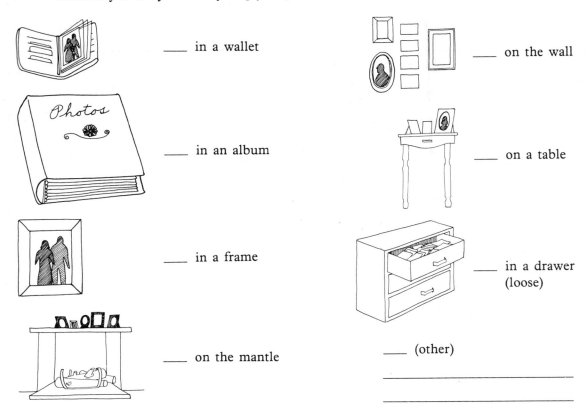

_____ in a wallet

_____ on the wall

_____ in an album

_____ on a table

_____ in a frame

_____ in a drawer (loose)

_____ on the mantle

_____ (other)

_____

_____

Where Do You Keep Your Photos?

1   Are your photographs all in one place? Are they organized according to topic? Do you have a date and a title for each one? If you answered *yes* to these three questions, then you are probably a very organized person. If you answered *no*, then you might not be an organized person. Your photos, however, still give you a lot of pleasure.

2   Most people have some photos in their wallet. We keep photos of our loved ones there, or perhaps of our favorite pets. Most people also have a few photos in frames, such as photos of grandparents and parents. We keep framed photos on the wall or on a table or mantle. We can look at these photos all the time.

3   The very organized person has photos in an album. Each photo has a date and a title. The photo album is like a personal history. The unorganized person probably has an album, too, but there aren't many photos in it. The photos might be loose, in a drawer or in folders and boxes. Sometimes there are dates and names on the back of loose photos, but often the names and dates are lost.

4   Perhaps it doesn't matter[1] where you keep your photos. Our photos all have the same purpose, and that is to help us remember people, events, and places from our past.

---

[1]it doesn't matter (expr) = it isn't important

Answer the questions orally or in writing.

1. This article describes how people organize their photographs. How do you organize your photographs?

2. Do you think that it is a good idea to keep photos in an album? Explain your answer.

3. Some people don't collect photos. Why do you think they don't?

H. Read: Daguerre's Discovery

1   One day in 1839, a Frenchman named Louis Daguerre ran to his wife and cried, "I have seized[1] the light; I have arrested[2] its flight." Daguerre's wife thought that he was crazy.*

2   Daguerre wasn't crazy, however. He was excited because he had discovered a new way to make images. His pictures, called daguerreotypes, quickly became popular in Europe and the United States. For the first time, people could have pictures of themselves and their families.

3   Although daguerreotypes were an amazing discovery, they were very different from modern photography. The images were made directly on chemically treated metal or glass. The metal or glass was the finished photograph. Today, of course, photographs are made on special chemically treated paper.

4   It was not easy to have a picture taken with this new invention. In the following imaginary letter, one woman describes her experiences with the daguerreotype. From the letter, we can get a feeling for what it was like to have "your daguerreotype taken."

---

[1]to seize (v) = to catch, to grasp

[2]to arrest (v) = to stop (*Note:* This is not the same as to take someone into custody by law, although the meanings are related.)

*Cecil Beaton and Gail Buckland, *The Magic Image: The Genius of Photography from 1939 to the Present Day* (Boston: Little, Brown & Co., 1975), pp. 10, 11.

Paris
April 12, 1843

Dear Anna,

Our trip is nearly over. We are in Paris at last! It is such a beautiful and romantic city! But news about Paris can wait until the next letter. In this one, I must tell you about our experience yesterday.

All of Paris is talking about something called the daguerreotype, so Jack and I decided to see this new invention. It makes exact images of people on a metal plate. When Jack saw it, he said right away[3] that we must have our pictures taken. And so our experience began!

First, the daguerreotypist (a Mr. Portier) told us to sit on a small couch. Behind the couch were two strange iron objects. They looked frightening, like some torture device! Mr. Portier told us to rest our heads against the objects, which looked like clamps. Next he told us to be very quiet and still. Again and again, he said, "You must not move one muscle!" But this is impossible, I thought.

Anna, can you guess how long we sat still? One complete minute! Don't laugh. That probably seems like a very short time to you. But imagine—we couldn't move our mouths at all. This was very difficult, because I was nervous, so I felt like laughing. In addition, we had to look directly into the camera and not even blink our eyes! After about half a minute, my nose began to itch, but I couldn't scratch it. I was even afraid to breathe! Well, Anna, that one minute seemed like one hour. When Mr. Portier said, "It's finished; you can relax," I was so happy. The first thing I did was to scratch my nose.

Jack and I were eager to see the picture, but it was very disappointing. We both looked like large dolls, not humans. Our expressions are very stern—we look angry and cold. Still, it is amazing to see an image of yourself that is on a piece of metal, not in a mirror. I will show you the picture when I see you next.

I promise to write soon with more news.

Fondly,

Charlotte

Answer the questions orally or in writing.

1. Why do you think daguerreotypes became so popular?

2. In most daguerreotypes, the people are not smiling. From the description in the article and the letter, can you explain why people seldom smiled?

---

[3]right away (adv) = immediately

3. What was the purpose of the iron headrests?

4. Can you think of any ways in which the old daguerreotypes might be better than modern photographs?

THE WORD SECTION

A. Selective Reading: Underline Same Words

Directions: Read the word(s) or phrase(s) on the left. Underline the same words or phrases in the sentence(s).

>   EXAMPLE: tourists/camera: Most <u>tourists</u> carry a <u>camera</u> when they travel.

1. amateur photographers: People who take pictures for fun are called amateur photographers.

2. chemicals/clothing: In the past, chemicals often burned the photographers' clothing.

3. developed/sent: The factory developed the film and sent the camera back to you with new film inside.

4. forgot/wind/key: One amateur photographer, a past President of the United States, once forgot to wind the key to his camera.

5. Kodak/small/simple: The Kodak was a small, light camera that was simple to use.

6. early cameras/large and heavy: The early cameras that were used in the 1800's were both large and heavy.

B. Selective Reading: Underline Category Word

Directions: Read the line of words. Underline the word that names the category of the other words.

>   EXAMPLE: worried   happy   nervous   sad   <u>feelings</u>   relaxed

1. reading material   newspaper   magazine   book   brochure

2. taking pictures   fishing   activities   reading   writing

3. camera   film   photographic equipment   chemicals

4. airplane   transportation   car   bus   train   taxi

5. photographer   profession   painter   teacher   actor

6. pictures   snapshots   paintings   photographs   drawings

C. Analogies

Directions: Complete analogies 1–3 by choosing one of the four words. Complete analogies 4–6 by choosing your own word. Write the word in the blank. Remember: The pairs of words must show the same relationship.

EXAMPLE: teacher : teach   _*Student*_   : study
(choose a word)

1. food : refrigerator   _____ : photo album
   camera   film   photographs   chemicals

2. amateur : hobby   professional : _____
   job   money   photographer   expensive

3. notebook paper : notebook   film : _____
   develop   photograph   roll   chemical

4. _____ : car   Kodak : camera

5. chemistry : _____   mathematics : numbers

6. painter : Degas   actor : _____

D. Word Forms: *-er* Suffixes

Here is one more analogy to complete:

Write : writer   read : _____

You probably wrote *reader* next to *read*. A writer is someone who writes, so a reader is someone who reads. Notice that both *writer* and *reader* end with *-er*. When we add *-er* (and sometimes *-or*) to certain words, the meaning of the word often changes to "someone who ___" (writes, reads, etc.). Thus, a photographer is someone who photographs.

What is an inventor?   _____

What is a painter?   _____

What is a basketball player?   _____

Directions: Part A. In part A, write the word in the blank that means "someone who ___ ." Some of the words will end in *-er* and some will end in *-or*. Ask a classmate, a native speaker, or your teacher if you are not sure about spelling.

1. Someone who plays soccer is a _____ .

2. Someone who jogs is a _____ .

3. Someone who acts is an _____ .

4. Someone who directs is a _____ .

5. Someone who travels is a _____ .

6. Someone who rules is a _____ .

7. Someone who tells stories is a _____ .

8. Someone who speaks is a _____ .

Directions: Part B. Sit with two or three classmates. Together, read the list of famous people. Try to decide who the people are. Then write each person's occupation (job) on the line. The words will probably end with the letters *-er* or *-or*. If you and your classmates don't know who the people are, put a question mark (?) in the blank, then ask a native speaker to help you. (Note: you can also find many of the names in the back of a large dictionary.)

1. Ernest Hemingway   _____

2. Ansel Adams   _____

3. Akira Kurosawa   _____

4. Emily Brontë   _____

5. Pele   _____

6. Muhammad Ali   _____

7. Jean-Claude Killy   _____

8. Barbra Streisand   _____

9. Kareem Abdul-Jabbar   _____

10. Thomas Edison   _____

11. Indira Ghandi   _____

12. John Wayne   _____

13. Georgia O'Keeffe   _____

CHAPTER 6
Compatibility

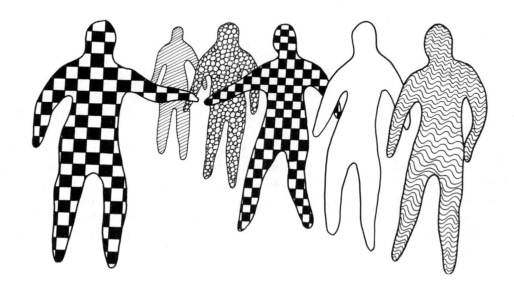

PREREADING ACTIVITIES

Part 1:   Likes and Dislikes

A.   Write the appropriate sports name under each picture. Look at the list of sports from Chart 1 in Section B if necessary.

_____   _____   _____

B.   Sit with a classmate (your partner for this activity). First, find all of the sports that you like very much on the chart on the next page. Add a sport if your favorite is not on the list. (Draw a picture of it in the blank square above if you wish). Put a 2 under the column YOU next to all of the sports that you like. Next, find all of the sports that you do not like at all. Put a 0 under the column YOU next to all of the sports that you dislike. If you feel neutral about a sport (neither like nor dislike), put a 1 on the chart in the appropriate box. Next, ask your partner the same information. Fill in the chart under the column YOUR PARTNER with 2's (like), 1's (neutral), and 0's (dislike).

2 = like   1 = feel neutral   0 = dislike

CHART 1: SPORTS			
	You	Your Partner	Row Totals
Baseball			
Football			
Basketball			
Soccer			
Tennis			
Volleyball			
Swimming			
Bowling			
Golf			
Jogging			
(Other) _____			
(Other) _____			

When the chart is complete for both you and your partner, sum the *rows* and write the totals in the right-hand column (ROW TOTALS). How many 4's are in your ROW TOTALS column? Number of 4's: ____ . How many 0's? Number of 0's ____ . If you have a lot of 4's and 0's, you and your partner like and dislike the same sports.

C. The next chart is similar to Chart 1. This time, you will write 2's next to foods that you like, 0's next to foods that you dislike, and 1's next to foods that you feel neutral about. (You and your partner may add some foods to this list.) Then fill in the chart with information about your partner's likes and dislikes.

2 = like   1 = feel neutral   0 = dislike

CHART 2: FOOD			
	You	Your Partner	Row Totals
Steak			
Fish			
Hamburgers			
Pizza			
Anchovies			
Bread			
Salad			
Ice Cream			
Fruit			
Garlic			
Rice			
Cheese			
(Other) _____			
(Other) _____			

When the chart is complete with information about you and your partner, sum the *rows* and write the totals in the column on the right. Again, count how many 4's and how many 0's you have. Number of 4's: _____ . Number of 0's: _____ . If you have a lot of 4's and 0's, you and your partner like and dislike similar foods.

D. Finally, complete the last chart, which asks you about your likes and dislikes in music. The music can be from your country or from the United States. (Note: If you and your classmates are not familiar with any of the music on the list, and if your teacher does not have some examples of this music, you may omit* Chart 3.)

    2 = like   1 = feel neutral   0 = dislike

_____

*to omit (v) = to leave out; if you *omit* a section, you do not do it.

CHART 3: MUSIC	You	Your Partner	Row Totals
Folk Music			
Rock			
Country & Western			
Classical			
Jazz			
Blues			
(Other) _____			
(Other) _____			

Sum the rows, and write the totals in the column on the right. Number of 4's: ____ .
Number of 0's: ____ . Do you and your partner like and dislike similar kinds of music?

Part 2:   Finding Compatible Classmates

If you and another person are **compatible**, it means that you can exist together harmoniously (without conflicts and problems). People can be compatible in many ways. One way is if they like and dislike similar things.

Problem: Find the person or people in your class with whom you are the most compatible, according to the information on your charts.

Solution: Look at the YOU column on your chart. (You will not be using the PART-NER column in this activity.) Your task is to find the people in your class who have their 2's, 1's, and 0's in the same boxes as you do. Therefore, you will need to compare your chart to your classmates' charts.
  Here are some suggestions: (a) Compare one chart only (sports *or* food *or* music). (b) Try to find at least one "compatible" person within 10 minutes. (c) Move freely around the class. (d) Look carefully at the charts of your classmates in the correct column (YOU). (e) Ask: "What do you have for [swimming]?" Answer: "I have (2)."
When you find some compatible classmates, write their names here:

_____

_____

_____

_____

Sit with your compatible classmates and discuss briefly the likes and dislikes from the other chart(s). Are you compatible according to your other charts?

Part 3: Survey and Predict

Read the list of key words. Then look quickly at the reading article that begins on page 120. Notice the beginning and the end of the article. Look quickly at each paragraph. In each paragraph, try to find several content words (nouns, verbs, adjectives) that you recognize.

True or False?   The reading article in this chapter is in the form of a personal letter.

   T   F

What kinds of words will you problably find in the article? Put a check next to your answers:

_____ Words about food

_____ Words about holidays and vacations

_____ Words about business

_____ Words about music

_____ Words about sports

_____ Words about cars

_____ Words about movies

_____ Words about love

_____ Words about photography

_____ Words about animals

Key Words

letter	differences	photography
to get married	athletic	to be friends
love	routines	to like (+ n)
compatible	breakfast	to like to (+ v)
veterinarian	lunch	
musician	dinner	

READING ARTICLE: The Letter: A Question of Compatibility

A.   THE LETTER: A QUESTION OF COMPATIBILITY   By Paragraph

BEFORE YOU BEGIN: You learned the word *compatible* in the Prereading Activity. This word is an adjective. *Compatibility* is the noun form of this word.

THINK AHEAD: This reading article is a letter from a woman, Angelina, to her fiancé (i.e., the man she is planning to marry). Can you guess what she might talk about in her letter? (Hint: Think about the title of the chapter.) If you have some ideas, write them here:

_____

_____

The Letter

October 3

Dear David,

1   Yesterday I received a very special letter from you. In it you said that you are finally ready to get married. After two years! It's about time, I said to myself. At first I was very happy. But then my common sense[1] made me stop and think very seriously. I decided to write you a letter. Here are my thoughts.

2   I love you, David, you know that. You love me. I know that. But is love enough to keep us together? Let's be realistic about our relationship. Are we really compatible?

FROM THE ARTICLE: From the first two paragraphs we get the idea that

Angelina ____ .
- a. is ready to get married
- b. is not sure about getting married
- c. is compatible with David

THINK AHEAD: In the next part of her letter, Angelina will probably talk

about ____ .
- a. differences between her and David
- b. similarities between her and David
- c. marriage plans

---

[1]common sense (n, U, expr) = practical intelligence, i.e., intelligence gained from experience, not from books

3   In the first place, I'm a veterinarian. I take care of dogs and cats. Animals are my life. You don't like pets, in particular dogs and cats, probably because you're allergic to them. You're a musician. Music is your life. You play beautiful music, I'm sure. But I'm tone-deaf.[2] I can't appreciate your music as well as other people can. I work during the day. You practice your music during the day and give concerts in the evening. These differences are facts about our lives. Will we ever see each other if we get married?

4   We also have some personal differences. For example, I'm athletic; you're not. In many ways, this difference is not important, of course. But just imagine how we will spend out weekends. I like to go jogging on Saturdays. Will you go with me? Probably not. You like to spend Sundays listening to classical music. Will I listen to music with you on Sundays? Probably not. I don't care for[3] classical music (even though I care for you). I prefer jazz. Plus,[4] I like to play golf or tennis on Sundays. You don't like golf at all. It's true that you like tennis, but your favorite tennis game is on TV, not on the tennis court.

FROM THE ARTICLE AND FROM YOUR KNOWLEDGE: In the last two paragraphs, Angelina talked about many differences between her and David. Which of these differences do you think is important? In other words, which differences might cause problems if they get married? Check as many as you want:

Job differences ☐

Feelings about animals ☐

Interest in sports ☐

Ways they like to spend their time on weekends ☐

Likes and dislikes in music ☐

THINK AHEAD: What do you think Angelina will talk about next? ____
   a. Similarities between her and David
   b. More differences between her and David
   c. Love and marriage

---

5   How about our daily routines? I go to bed early and get up early. Even on weekends I like to get up at 7:00. You sleep late and get up late. How can we have breakfast to-

---

[2]tone-deaf (adj) = not able to distinguish different notes in music

[3]I don't care for _____ (expr) = I don't like _____ (polite)

[4]plus (adv) = in addition, moreover (conversational)

gether? Speaking of breakfast, you eat a heavy breakfast—eggs, bacon, toast, and fruit. I don't like a heavy breakfast. I prefer coffee and toast. You don't eat lunch, because you have a big, late breakfast. I'm starved[5] by lunchtime. I like to eat a huge lunch. My favorite lunch is a big hot sandwich, a salad, and a bowl of soup. You get hungry for dinner by 5:30, because you don't eat lunch. I like to relax after I get home from work and eat later, at 7:00 or 8:00.

6   Maybe those differences are not so important either. But how about these? You live in New York; I live in California. You need to travel for your job; I can't travel because of my job. Your mother doesn't like me; my mother doesn't like you. You want an apartment in the city; I want a house in the country. You squeeze the toothpaste from the bottom; I squeeze it from the middle. David, how can we have a compatible marriage?

FROM THE ARTICLE AND FROM YOUR KNOWLEDGE: In paragraphs 5 and 6, Angelina discusses many more differences. Which one do you think is the most important?

_____

Which one do you think is the least important?

_____

FROM YOUR KNOWLEDGE AND THINK AHEAD: From the information you have so far about Angelina and David, do you think they should get married?

Yes ☐   No ☐   I don't know; I need more information. ☐

---

7   Well, I guess we have a few things in common. We're both[6] in our 40s.[7] We were both married once before. We both like photography. In fact, you're a pretty good photographer. I like to take photos of animals, understandably. I enclosed a photo in this letter

---

[5]starved (also—starving) (adj) = very hungry (conversational)

[6]both (adj and pn) = two of two

[7]to be in one's 40s (v, expr) = to be between the ages of 40 and 49

of some elephant seals at Año Nuevo beach. What do you think of it? Perhaps after we get married, we can build a darkroom.[8] Do you like that idea? We also both love pizza with anchovies. Most of my other friends hate anchovies. If we don't get married, who will I eat pizza with? We both like to cook, too, and to eat good food. And we both like to see good movies and read good books. Both of us dislike politics and politicians. Most important, we're both honest. We don't lie. We can talk openly and comfortably. David, I trust you and I love you! What should we do? What should I do? Should I say yes? Should I say no? Should we get married? Should we just be friends? Should we be married *and* be friends?

8   I will write you again soon. Meanwhile, please write me back a.s.a.p.[9] What do you think? Are we compatible?

   With love,

   Angelina

FROM THE ARTICLE: How are Angelina and David similar? List several areas. (They both like ____ ; they both dislike ____ .)

_____

_____

_____

_____

_____

FROM YOUR KNOWLEDGE: Are Angelina and David compatible? Should they get married?

   Yes ☐   No ☐   I can't decide. ☐

---

[8]darkroom (n, C) = a room where photographers can develop film and print photographs

[9]a.s.a.p. (expr) = "as soon as possible" (conversational)

B. THE LETTER: A QUESTION OF COMPATIBILITY   Complete Reading

October 3

Dear David,

1   Yesterday I received a very special letter from you. In it you said that you are finally ready to get married. After two years! It's about time, I said to myself. At first I was very happy. But then my common sense made me stop and think very seriously. I decided to write you a letter. Here are my thoughts.

2   I love you, David, you know that. You love me. I know that. But is love enough to keep us together? Let's be realistic about our relationship. Are we really compatible?

3   In the first place, I'm a veterinarian. I take care of dogs and cats. Animals are my life. You don't like pets, in particular dogs and cats, probably because you're allergic to them. You're a musician. Music is your life. You play beautiful music, I'm sure. But I'm tone-deaf. I can't appreciate your music as well as other people can. I work during the day. You practice your music during the day and give concerts in the evening. These differences are facts about our lives. Will we ever see each other if we get married?

4   We also have some personal differences. For example, I'm athletic; you're not. In many ways, this difference is not important, of course. But just imagine how we will spend our weekends. I like to go jogging on Saturdays. Will you go with me? Probably not. You like to spend Sundays listening to classical music. Will I listen to music with you on Sundays? Probably not. I don't care for classical music (even though I care for you). I prefer jazz. Plus, I like to play golf or tennis on Sundays. You don't like golf at all. It's true that you like tennis, but your favorite tennis game is on TV, not on the tennis court.

5   How about our daily routines? I go to bed early and get up early. Even on weekends I like to get up at 7:00. You sleep late and get up late. How can we have breakfast together? Speaking of breakfast, you eat a heavy breakfast—eggs, bacon, toast, and fruit. I don't like a heavy breakfast. I prefer coffee and toast. You don't eat lunch, because you have a big, late breakfast. I'm starved by lunchtime. I like to eat a huge lunch. My favorite lunch is a big hot sandwich, a salad, and a bowl of soup. You get hungry for dinner by 5:30, because you don't eat lunch. I like to relax after I get home from work and eat later, at 7:00 or 8:00.

6   Maybe those differences are not so important either. But how about these? You live in New York; I live in California. You need to travel for your job; I can't travel because of my job. Your mother doesn't like me; my mother doesn't like you. You want an apartment in the city; I want a house in the country. You squeeze the toothpaste from the bottom; I squeeze it from the middle. David, how can we have a compatible marriage?

7   Well, I guess we have a few things in common. We're both in our 40s. We were both married once before. We both like photography. In fact, you're a pretty good photographer. I like to take photos of animals, understandably. I enclosed a photo in this letter of some elephant seals at Año Nuevo beach. What do you think of it? Perhaps after we

get married, we can build a darkroom. Do you like that idea? We also both love pizza with anchovies. Most of my other friends hate anchovies. If we don't get married, who will I eat pizza with? We both like to cook, too, and to eat good food. And we both like to see good movies and read good books. Both of us dislike politics and politicians. Most important, we're both honest. We don't lie. We can talk openly and comfortably. David, I trust you and I love you! What should we do? What should I do? Should I say yes? Should I say no? Should we get married? Should we just be friends? Should we be married *and* be friends?

8   I will write you again soon. Meanwhile, please write me back a.s.a.p. What do you think? Are we compatible?

With love,

Angelina

Comprehension Questions

Answer the questions orally or in writing.

1. Make a list of some of the topics that Angelina discussed in her letter. They can be in any order; just try to remember as many as you can.

   _____   _____

   _____   _____

   _____   _____

   _____   _____

2. What hobby do Angelina and David have in common?
   a. Playing tennis
   b. Listening to classical music
   c. Photography

3. What do you think Angelina will do? ____
   a. She will probably agree to marry David.
   b. She will probably decide not to marry David.
   c. She will probably let David decide what to do.

4. Compare your likes and dislikes with those of Angelina and David. Who are you more similar to?

   I am more similar to Angelina. ☐

   I am more similar to David. ☐

   I am very different from both of them. ☐

5. If Angelina and David get married, what do you think they need to do in order to have a successful marriage? Write your ideas or discuss them in class.

EXERCISES AND FURTHER READINGS

A. Reference

Directions: Read the sentences. The underlined words refer to a noun phrase in one of the earlier sentences. Write the phrase in the blank. (Note: One of the underlined words is an adverb. It refers to a place.)

> EXAMPLE: Angelina has two sisters. She likes both of them a lot.
>
> SHE = _Angelina_
>
> THEM = _(two) sisters_

1. Angelina's home town is a suburb of Los Angeles. It is near Disneyland, but, surprisingly, Angelina has never been there .

    IT = _____

    THERE = _____

2. One of Angelina's sisters likes pizza with everything on it—cheese, vegetables, meat. However, she doesn't like anchovies, so she never orders them .

    IT = _____

    SHE = _____

    SHE = _____

    THEM = _____

3. David and Angelina are very different, but they both like photography. It represents a common interest.

    THEY = _____

    IT = _____

4. David likes tennis, but he hates golf. He doesn't like to play it , or even to watch it on TV. He finds the game very boring.

    HE = _____

    HE = _____

    IT = _____

    IT = _____

    HE = _____

    THE GAME = _____

5. Olympic athletes train (= practice their sport) for four years. For <u>them</u> , athletics is similar to a full-time job. <u>It</u> requires many hours every day of energy and concentration. <u>Some</u> , however, have regular jobs or go to school while <u>they</u> are training.

THEM = _____

IT = _____

SOME = _____

THEY = _____

6. A pen pal is a special person. <u>He or she</u> is a friend that we have not met—<u>one</u> that we write letters to on a friendly basis.

HE OR SHE = _____

ONE = _____

B. Grammatical Word Groups: Identify

Directions: Read the word group in parentheses. Then underline the word groups that have a similar grammatical structure.

EXAMPLE: (a pizza)   <u>some bread</u>   in the refrigerator   <u>an apple</u>   some an-chovies   eat a pizza   <u>the cheese</u>

EXPLANATION: The word group *a pizza* consists of a determiner (*a*) and a noun (*pizza*). Several other groups in the list consist of a determiner plus a noun: *some bread, an apple, some anchovies,* and *the cheese.* The other groups do not belong with the group "determiner plus noun."

1. (in this letter)   at the office   in my family   several large pizzas   at a photo store   write a letter

2. (classical music)   small dog   boring game   sleeping children   hates anchovies   sad music

3. (on the weekends)   with a friend   the daily routine   in an animal hospital   working part-time   in the country

4. (very nice)   to discuss it   extremely compatible   large meal   too different   really beautiful   somewhat tone-deaf

C. Grammatical Word Groups: Read

Directions: Read the paragraph about pen pals quickly three times—once with vertically spaced grammatical word groups, once with horizontally spaced word groups, and once with normal spacing.

1. Vertical

Pen pals

are special kinds of friends.

They are friends

who live far away,

perhaps in a different country.

We get to know pen pals

by writing letters to them

and receiving letters back

(hence the name *pen* pal).

Many pen pals

have never met each other.

They have become friends

simply by exchanging letters

over many years.

Do you have a pen pal?

2. Horizontal

Pen pals   are special kinds of friends.   They are friends   who live far away, perhaps in a different country.   We get to know pen pals   by writing letters to them and receiving letters back   (hence the name *pen* pal).   Many pen pals   have never met each other.   They have become friends   simply by exchanging letters   over many years.   Do you have a pen pal?

3. Normal Spacing

Pen pals are special kinds of friends. They are friends who live far away, perhaps in a different country. We get to know pen pals by writing letters to them and receiving letters back (hence the name *pen* pal). Many pen pals have never met each other. They have become friends simply by exchanging letters over many years. Do you have a pen pal?

D. Order

Directions: Read the sentences. They give some information about the life of Elizabeth Barrett Browning, the English poet (1806–1861). The sentences are not in a logical order. Put a number next to each sentence to show a better order.

Elizabeth Barrett Browning

_____ As a result, in part, of this accident, and because of bad lungs, she was not healthy for the rest of her life.

_____ She was a happy, intelligent child.

_____ They lived happily until her death in 1861.

_____ By the age of twelve, she could read Greek and write poetry.

_____ Elizabeth Barrett Browning, the English poet, was born in 1806.

_____ When she was almost forty, however, a wonderful thing happened.

_____ She also loved to ride horses as a child.

_____ She was badly injured.

_____ She met and fell in love with the famous poet Robert Browning.

_____ Sadly, at the age of fifteen, she fell while she was taking care of her horse.

_____ She married him in 1846.

E. Agree/Disagree

Directions: Circle **A** if you agree with the statements. Circle **D** if you disagree. Discuss your opinions with your classmates.

	Agree	*Disagree*
1. People must be compatible in most ways in order to be happily married.	A	D
2. People should not spend money on veterinarians and medicines for their pets.	A	D
3. People who like dogs usually don't like cats.	A	D
4. Baseball is an interesting sport.	A	D

5. Mothers should stay home with their children.   A   D

6. Classical music is more beautiful than rock music.   A   D

7. Most rock music is too loud.   A   D

F. Getting Information from a Native Speaker

In her letter, Angelina described differences and similarities between her and David. She was not sure which differences and similarities were important and which were not important to the success of a marriage. Do you think that it is important for married couples to agree on everything?

Directions: Look at the list of topics below. Which things are most important for couples to agree on? Which things are not so important? First, talk with a classmate, then fill in your answers. Do you and your classmate agree?

	Important to Agree On		*Not Important to Agree On*	
	You	*Native Speaker*	*You*	*Native Speaker*
1. Eating habits	⎯	⎯	⎯	⎯
2. Daily schedule	⎯	⎯	⎯	⎯
3. Politics	⎯	⎯	⎯	⎯
4. Religion	⎯	⎯	⎯	⎯
5. Taste in music	⎯	⎯	⎯	⎯
6. Free-time activities	⎯	⎯	⎯	⎯
7. Where to live (city, country, house, apartment, etc.)	⎯	⎯	⎯	⎯
8. (Other) _____	⎯	⎯	⎯	⎯

Now show the list of topics to a native speaker of English. Explain that you are doing a cross-cultural survey on ideas about marriage. Ask: "Is it important for couples to agree on _____ ?" Record the native speaker's answers next to your answers. Discuss your results with your classmates.

G. Read: A Memo from the Foreign Student Advisor

MEMORANDUM

To: All Foreign Students and their Instructors

From: Mrs. Barth, Foreign Student Advisor

Date: Nov. 1

Re: Applications to Universities

(1) Planning to attend a 4-year university or graduate school next year? If so, application deadlines for many universities are at the end of this month. University catalogues and application forms are in my office. IMPORTANT: FIND THE UNIVERSITY THAT IS RIGHT FOR YOU!

(2) IMPORTANT—You may need to take TOEFL[1] and SAT[2]. Grad students may need TOEFL and GRE[3]. REGISTER NOW for test dates.

(3) Need help with applications? Make an appointment with me any time M–F, 1–5.

(4) Apply now! Late applications are not accepted at many universities!

Answer the questions orally or in writing.
This is a "memo" (memorandum). A memo is an informal written communication from an office at a business or at a school. Is all of the information in this memo written in complete sentences?

1. Who wrote this memo?

2. Who is the memo for?

3. What students will be interested in reading this memo?

4. When are applications due at many universities? Give the month and date.

5. What is a "grad student"?

---

[1]TOEFL = Test of English as a Foreign Language

[2]SAT = Scholastic Aptitude Test

[3]GRE = Graduate Record Examination

6. How many tests might foreign students need to take before going to an American university?

7. When can foreign students see the advisor in her office?

8. If you want to go to a university, how many months ahead of time should you apply?

9. Mrs. Barth says in this memo: "Find the university that is right for you." What does she mean by this advice? Can a student and a university be compatible or incompatible? Discuss these questions with your classmates.

H. Read: Matchmaking

Prereading

Men and women from every culture enjoy meeting each other. But the places where men and women can meet might be different in different cultures. Where do single (i.e., not married) men and women meet in your culture? (Note: *Meet* in this context means to meet someone for the first time *and* to meet someone regularly.) Look at the chart. Check the appropriate boxes to show how often men and women meet at each place.

FREQUENCY

PLACE	Never	Sometimes	Usually	Always
At a party				
At church, temple, or mosque				
At work				
At the parents' home				
At a bar				
Other: _____				
Other: _____				

Compare your chart with the charts of your classmates. Are there similarities and differences according to cultures?

Now continue the reading:

In certain cultures, men and women sometimes meet each other for the first time with the help of a special computerized business. This business tries to match men and women who have similar likes and dislikes. For this reason, it is called a "Match-Making Service," or a "Computer Dating Service." People who go to a matchmaking service usually pay a fee and fill out a form with some personal information. (See the example below.) The matchmaking service provides these people with a list of names and telephone numbers of other people with similar likes and interests.

Look at the example form. Then read the four filled-out forms that follow. Try to be a "matchmaker." Choose one man and one woman who will probably be compatible. Be ready to explain your answer.

MATCHMAKING INFORMATION FORM (Example):

Name _____ Sex _____ Age _____

Telephone number _____

Occupation _____

Hobbies _____

Favorite time of day/free time _____

_____

Do you like children? Yes ☐   No ☐

Describe your "Perfect Date" activities: _____

_____

_____

---

1. Name: Muriel   F   Age: 31

   Occupation: real estate agent

   Hobbies: bicycling, going to movies

   Time: morning

   Children: not really

   Perfect date: an early morning bike ride, followed by a picnic brunch

2. Name: George   M   Age: 53

Occupation: electrician

Hobbies: bowling, baseball (fan, not player)

Time: evening

Children: yes

Perfect date: dinner out, and then bowling or a movie; or (better yet) a baseball game

3. Name: Carol   F   Age: 43

Occupation: investment consultant

Hobbies: reading, dancing

Time: after dark

Children: yes

Perfect date: dinner out and dancing till dawn

4. Name: Leonard   M   age: 33

Occupation: banker

Hobbies: travel, cooking, music

Time: evening

Children: yes

Perfect date: dinner at home, then go to the symphony

Who belongs together? _____ and _____

How did you decide who belongs together? Do you and your classmates agree?

I. Read: The World's Most Compatible Pen Pals: A True Love Story*

1   Elizabeth Barrett Browning (1806–1861) and Robert Browning (1812–1889) were both English poets. The story of how they met, fell in love, and married is one of the most famous love stories in history. This love story is famous for is purity, its poetry, and its passion. But most of all, it is famous because their romance took place[1] primarily by mail. For the two years before they married, they wrote to each other almost every day.

---

[1] to take place (v) = to occur, to happen

* The information for this reading is taken from Frances Winwar, *The Immortal Lovers: Elizabeth Barrett and Robert Browning* (New York: Harper & Row, 1950).

2   Elizabeth Barrett lived a quiet life in the house of her father. She rarely left the house because she was very weak and sick with a lung disease. From childhood she spent her time reading, studying Greek, and writing poetry. Her poems were published and became popular both in England and in America.

3   Elizabeth's father, Mr. Barrett, supported his daughter's writing. However, he was very strict and also eccentric[2]—he refused to let any of his three daughters marry. He wanted them all to stay with him. When Elizabeth was thirty-seven, she still lived with her father and her two unmarried sisters. She had never married or even been in love. She lived in a dream world. She knew Robert Browning only by name. However, she read his poetry and admired it greatly. She even put his name in a poem that she wrote.

4   Robert Browning's childhood was similar to Elizabeth's. He studied Greek, read a great deal, and wrote poetry at a very young age. As a young adult, he continued to read and write, and struggled to publish his work. By the age of thirty, he was not yet married. One day, he was reading some of Elizabeth's poems. He admired her poetry very much. Suddenly, he saw his name in one of her poems. He was so surprised and pleased that he decided to write her a letter. The year was 1844.

5   With this letter, Elizabeth Barrett and Robert Browning began a secret correspondence.[3] They wrote to each other almost every day. At first, their letters were formal and impersonal. They discussed poetry and literature. Slowly, the letters became more personal. A friendship developed as they discovered their common interests and ideas. They read and criticized each other's poetry and began to discuss their friendship. They seemed to be perfectly compatible, both intellectually and spiritually. After one year, Robert wrote to Elizabeth that he loved her. They still had never met each other.

6   Finally, Elizabeth and Robert arranged to meet while Elizabeth's father was not in the house. They were nervous, and even shocked, to see each other face to face at last. They continued meeting and talking secretly once or twice a week for the next year. They also continued to write each other letters every day. Elizabeth wrote: ". . . . You cannot guess what you are to me—you cannot—it is not possible. . . . It is something to me between dream and miracle." Robert wrote: "I never in my life kept a journal. . . . But I have, from the first, recorded the date and duration of every visit to you; the number of minutes you have given me, and I put them together till they make—nearly two days now; four-and-twenty-hour long days, that I have been by you. . . ."

7   Then, in September, 1846, in a secret marriage ceremony, Elizabeth Barrett became Elizabeth Barrett Browning. A week later, without telling Elizabeth's father, the happy couple eloped[4] to Italy. The shock was terrible for Mr. Barrett, but his anger could not

---

[2]eccentric (adj) = very different and strange

[3]correspondence (n, U) = communication by letters

[4]to elope (v) = to run away and be secretly married

diminish their happiness. In 1849, they succeeded in having a son. They lived in Italy, ecstatically happy, for fifteen years, until Elizabeth's death in 1861.

Discuss the following questions with your classmates.

1. Mr. Barrett, Elizabeth's father, was an eccentric man. He did not want his daughters *or* his sons to marry. Therefore, Elizabeth and Robert corresponded and married secretly. Were they right or wrong not to tell Mr. Barrett about their love?

2. Can you imagine any reasons why Mr. Barrett did not want his children to marry? (Note: Nobody knows the real answer for certain.)

3. Elizabeth and Robert spent very little time together before they married. They learned about each other primarily through their letters. Do you think this is a good way to get to know someone? What are some advantages and disadvantages (good and bad things) about a friendship that develops through letters? Is it better to get to know someone face to face?

4. Elizabeth and Robert married quite late—she was thirty-nine and he was thirty-three. What are some advantages and disadvantages of marrying late? What are some advantages and disadvantages of marrying very young?

THE WORD SECTION

A. Selective Reading: Cross Out Unrelated Word

Directions: Read the group of words. Cross out the word that does not belong in the group. When you finish, explain your decisions to your classmates.

> EXAMPLE: fiancés   pen pals   friends   ~~brothers~~   classmates
>
> EXPLANATION: Brothers are blood relatives. The other words describe relationships that are not related by blood.

1. college   high school   university   home town   community college

2. veterinarians   musicians   writers   athletes   sports   teachers

3. weekdays   evenings   mornings   weekends   routines

4. friends   marriage   partners   roommates   cousins

5. classical   tone-deaf   jazz   rock   blues

B.   Selective Reading: Underline Examples

Directions: Look at the general category word on the left. Then read the sentence(s). Underline all examples or descriptions of the general category word in the sentence.

> EXAMPLE: (relatives)   David has one <u>brother</u> and one <u>sister</u>. His <u>mother</u> and <u>father</u> are retired and living in New York.

1. (sports)   Popular winter sports are skiing and ice-skating. Summer sports include swimming, tennis, and baseball.

2. (kinds of music)   Some large universities have their own radio stations. The radio programs play a variety of music such as classical, jazz, folk, and rock.

3. (meals)   People who eat a late, heavy breakfast sometimes omit lunch. They have a large dinner instead.

4. (pets)   In the United States and other Western countries, dogs, cats, and birds live inside people's houses and are treated like members of the family.

5. (big cities)   Los Angeles and New York City are crowded, smoggy, and noisy. San Francisco is less smoggy because it is near the ocean and less industrial than Los Angeles or the East Coast.

C.   Levels of Generalization

Directions: Read each group of words and phrases. One word or phrase in each group is *general* (**G**). Another word or phrase is *specific* (**S**). The remaining words or phrases are *more specific* examples (**MS**) of the specific category. Write **G, S** or **MS** before the appropriate words and phrases.

> EXAMPLE: <u>S</u> carbohydrates
> <u>MS</u> bread
> <u>G</u> food
> <u>MS</u> rice
> <u>MS</u> potatoes

1. ___ breakfast

___ food

___ toast

___ eggs

___ fruit

2. ___ letters to friends

___ love letters

___ written material

___ business letters

___ correspondence

3. ___ penny

___ nickel

___ coins

___ money

___ quarter

___ dime

4. ___ reading material

___ textbook

___ book

___ cookbook

___ novel

5. ___ Chopin

___ Bach

___ classical music

___ Debussy

___ Beethoven

___ music

D. Antonyms

The letter in this chapter describes many differences between Angelina and David. They are opposite in many ways. The list of words and phrases below is based on Angelina's letter to David.

Directions: With one or two classmates, write a word or phrase in each blank that has an opposite meaning from the word or phrase in the list. Note: You will need to use your own knowledge of vocabulary as well as vocabulary from the letter. You may write more than one antonym. There are several good answers.

EXAMPLE: love (n) _____*hate*_____

1. early (adv) _____
2. city (n) _____
3. starved (adj) _____
4. to like (v) _____
5. to divorce (v) _____
6. athletic (adj) _____
7. to have a good ear (v)

    (= to hear musical notes accurately) _____
8. different (adj) _____
9. huge (adj) _____
10. to go to bed (v) _____
11. to send a letter (v) _____
12. married (adj) _____
13. weekday (n) _____
14. to work hard (v) _____

CHAPTER 7
The Health Clinic

PREREADING ACTIVITIES

Part 1A: Stress Survey

Complete the stress survey on the next page by checking the appropriate boxes and circling the appropriate numbers.

STRESS SURVEY

1. How many times a day do you eat?   1 2 3 4

2. Do you think that you eat healthy food?
   Yes ☐   No ☐   Sometimes ☐

3. Do you ever get stomachaches?
   Often ☐   Sometimes ☐   Rarely ☐   Never ☐

4. Do you ever feel nervous?
   Often ☐   Sometimes ☐   Rarely ☐   Never ☐

5. If you answered *Often* or *Sometimes* to question 4, please try to describe the situation(s) in which you feel nervous:

   I feel nervous when: _____

   _____

   _____

6. How many hours a night do you sleep? (Circle one)
   4 5 6 7 8 9 9+

7. How many hours a day do you study? (Circle one)
              Less than one   1–2   2–3   3–4   4+

8. Are you experiencing any academic pressure? (Are you worried about your studies?)
   Yes, a lot ☐   No, not much ☐   Some ☐

9. Are you feeling any pressures from parents, family, or work?
   Yes, a lot ☐   No, not much ☐   Some ☐

10. Do you ever get headaches?
    Often ☐   Sometimes ☐   Rarely ☐   Never ☐

11. Do you play any sports or do any exercise?
    Often ☐   Sometimes ☐   Rarely ☐   Never ☐

Now share your Stress Surveys with several classmates. Are your answers similar? Different?

Part 1B: The Possible Causes of Stomachaches and Headaches

In this activity, you will discuss the possible causes of two health problems: stomachaches and headaches. There are many "correct" answers. The idea is to think of as many answers as possible. Of course, your answers must be plausible (they must make sense, be possible).

Directions: Sit with 3–5 classmates. Choose one person to take notes. As a group, think of as many possible answers as you can. The note-taker should write your group's answers on a separate piece of paper. (Use the spaces below for your own ideas.)

Question 1:   Why do people get stomachaches? List as many causes as you can think of:

_____

_____

_____

_____

_____

_____

Question 2:   Why do people get headaches? List as many causes as you can think of:

_____

_____

_____

_____

When your group is finished, ask one person to be the reporter. The reporters should share each group's ideas with the whole class. Which ideas are common among all the groups? Which ideas are unique (i.e., only 1 group has the idea)?

Part 2:   Health Clinic Services

Many universities have student health clinics. A health clinic is similar to a hospital or a doctor's office in some ways. For example, if you feel sick, you can go to the health clinic. A doctor will examine you. If your problem is minor (simple, not serious), the health clinic can help you. If the problem is more serious, the health clinic can give you advice and help you find another doctor.

A. Read the list of services from the chart below. Some of the services are usually provided by student health clinics. Other services are not usually provided by these clinics. With several other classmates, try to decide which services are usually provided by student health clinics and which are not. Put a check in the appropriate box of the chart.

SERVICES	Provided by Health Clinics	Not Provided by Health Clinics
Blood Tests		
X-rays		
Eye Tests		
Information about Health		
Dental Care		
Prenatal Care		
Surgery		
Psychological Counseling		
Cancer Therapy		
Prescriptions		

B. Do you have a health center at your school?   Yes ☐   No ☐

1. If you answered Yes:
  What services does your health center provide? (Note: If you are not sure, visit your health center before you complete this question.)

_____

_____

_____

_____

2. If you answered No, where do students go for medical care? Ask your classmates. (Check as many answers as are appropriate.)

_____ Health centers or health clinics in the city

_____ Private doctors

_____ A hospital in the city

_____ (Other: describe) _____

C. Sit with several classmates. Discuss this question:

1. If university students in your country get sick, where do they go for care?

School health center ☐

Private doctor ☐

Hospital ☐

Family ☐

(Other) _____ ☐

2. What kinds of health problems do students often have in your country? (Check as many as are appropriate.)

Stomach problems ☐

Headaches ☐

Backaches ☐

Eye problems ☐

Teeth problems ☐

Accidents (broken bones, cuts, etc.) ☐

High blood pressure ☐

Skin problems ☐

(Other) _____ ☐

Are the health problems that students in your class have similar? If they are different, talk about some of the differences. Do you believe that students in all countries have some health problems that are similar? If you answered Yes, why do you think their health problems are similar?

Part 3:   Survey and Predict

Read the list of key words. Look at the reading article that begins on page 148. Read the title and the headings, and look at the photographs. What topics do you think you will read about in this article? Check as many answers as you believe are appropriate.

_____   Why people get colds and flu

_____   The people who work at health clinics

_____   The services provided by health clinics

_____   The description of specific illnesses

_____   The services that are not provided by health clinics

_____   The kinds of hospitals in the United States

_____   What happens when you have a blood test

Key Words

to feel (get, be) sick	stomachache	pharmacy
cold	minor	prescription
flu	major	medication
accident	to see a doctor	information
stress	laboratory	services
headache	fee	

READING ARTICLE: The Health Clinic

A.   THE HEALTH CLINIC By Paragraph

1   Everybody feels sick now and then. People get colds and respiratory flu, especially in winter. Sometimes they get a stomach flu or perhaps get sick from some bad food. Of course, it is possible to have a problem without being sick. People can have accidents that result in injuries—broken bones, injured muscles, cuts, and bruises. They can also feel sick because of stress and tension, which can cause headaches and stomachaches. Most health problems like these are not serious. They do not require us to go to a hospital.

2   A health clinic is a place where people can go if they have minor[1] medical problems. It is not a private doctor's practice, which is very expensive. Likewise, it is not a hospital, which takes care of major[2] medical problems. It consists of a group of doctors and nurses who have many offices in the same building. A visit to a health clinic is less expensive than a visit to a private doctor or a hospital.

3   Many universities have student health clinics (also called *health centers* or *health services*). All registered students can go there if they have minor health problems. For example, students go to the clinic if they have the flu, a bad cold, or an injury from a minor accident. Student athletes often use the university health clinic because they are sometimes hurt while playing their sports. Even the spouses[3] of registered students can use the university health services.

C. Pearson Casanave

4   University health clinics also take care of students with school-related health problems. Some examples of school-related health problems are stomachaches, headaches, and backaches. These problems are often caused by stress, when students feel tense and nervous during the school year. For example, at exam time, at the end of the term or the year, all students experience extra academic pressure. Too much academic pressure can cause health problems. Sometimes foreign students, however, also experience these problems during their first few months in a new country. The problems might be caused by stress from culture shock, by different food, and by not enough sleep. Students who feel sick because of culture shock or academic pressure can go to the university health clinic for help. Let us look more closely at the health clinic staff and services.

---

[1]minor (adj) = small; not important

[2]major (adj) = large; important

[3]spouses (n, C, pl) = husbands or wives

FROM THE ARTICLE: Think about the information in paragraphs 1–4. These paragraphs discuss three main causes of health problems. The three causes are ___ .

    a. headaches, stomachaches, and backaches
    b. sickness, accidents, and stress
    c. colds, flu, and bad food

FROM THE ARTICLE: According to the article, health clinics take care of ___ .

    a. minor health problems
    b. major health problems
    c. all health problems

FROM THE ARTICLE AND FROM YOUR KNOWLEDGE: Paragraphs 1–4 discuss several kinds of health problems. Which of these health problems have you experienced in the last twelve months? Make a list.

_____   _____

_____   _____

_____   _____

THINK AHEAD: Read the last sentence of paragraph 4. What does this sentence tell you? ___

    a. The next part of the reading is not going to discuss health clinics.
    b. The next part of the reading is going to discuss general information about health clinics.
    c. The next part of the reading is going to discuss specific information about health clinics.

Health Clinic Staff

5   Who works at the student health clinic? Several kinds of professional people usually work there: physicians, physicians' assistants (these may be graduate medical students), counselors, and nurses. These doctors, counselors, and nurses take care of your physical health (your body) and your mental health (your mind). You can see one of them by making an appointment by phone or in person. You can also walk in to the clinic and wait your turn. If you have an urgent problem (an emergency), you can usually see a doctor without waiting.

Special Services and Fees

6   University health clinics usually have laboratories and X-ray units. For example, you can get a blood test at the health clinic. You might need to pay a small laboratory fee for the test. Or perhaps you think that you cracked a bone while playing a sport. In this case, you can go to the health clinic for an X-ray. An X-ray might be free or it might cost a small amount of money. These fees, however, are much lower than the fees at a regular doctor's office.

C. Pearson Casanave

7   Some health clinics have their own pharmacies. If a health clinic doctor gives you a prescription for some medication, you can get your prescription at the clinic pharmacy. The medications at health clinic pharmacies are usually less expensive than medications at regular pharmacies. If the clinic does not have a pharmacy, then you need to pay the full price at a regular pharmacy for your prescription.

FROM THE ARTICLE: What were paragraphs 5–7 about? Write as many words and phrases as you can remember. Try NOT to look back at the paragraphs. Don't worry about spelling.

_____

_____

_____

FROM THE ARTICLE: The word _staff_ in the heading for paragraph 5 means ____ .

    a. doctors and nurses
    b. counselors
    c. students
    d. all the people who work at the health clinic

FROM YOUR KNOWLEDGE: In your country, when you go to a doctor, hospital, or clinic, what kind of fee do you pay? ____

    a. a high fee
    b. a low fee
    c. no fee

THINK AHEAD: Health clinics do not take care of all health problems. What problems _don't_ they take care of? Make some guesses.

_____

_____

_____

What the Health Clinic Does NOT Do

8   Student health clinics do not take care of all of your health problems. For example, they do not take care of your teeth. For dental problems, you need to see a dentist. Similarly, the clinic does not test your eyes or give you glasses. You need to visit an optometrist or an ophthalmologist for eye problems. Finally, student health clinics do not take care of major medical problems. You need to go to a regular doctor or a hospital for those. You can get the names of outside dentists and doctors from someone at the health clinic.

Staying Healthy

9   Health clinics take care of students who get sick. But students do not want to get sick. They want to stay healthy and stay *out* of the health clinic. Therefore, the clinic can give information to students about how to stay healthy. For example, health clinics usually have information about food and diet, about common illnesses, and about tension and stress (a common student health problem). This information is printed in individual brochures and pamphlets or in booklets. The brochures and booklets are free.

10   In conclusion, health clinics provide important services for students. Students help to pay for these services with their registration fees. If you are a student on a university campus, find out what the health center can do for you. If you do not have a health clinic on your campus, find out if there is one in your city. Learn about the health services that are available to you.

FROM THE ARTICLE: Sometimes healthy people (people who are not sick) go to a health clinic. Why?

_____

_____

FROM THE ARTICLE: *Optometrists* and *ophthalmologists* are ____ .

    a. professional people
    b. medicines
    c. health problems

FROM YOUR KNOWLEDGE: Check all the places that have a health clinic.

    ____ The school where you are studying English now

    ____ The city where you are living now

    ____ Your high school, university, or company in your home country

    ____ Your hometown

    ____ (Other) _____

_____

B. THE HEALTH CLINIC Complete Reading

1   Everybody feels sick now and then. People get colds and respiratory flu, especially in the winter. Sometimes they get a stomach flu or perhaps get sick from some bad food. Of course, it is possible to have a problem without being sick. People can have accidents that result in injuries—broken bones, injured muscles, cuts, and bruises. They can also feel sick because of stress and tension, which can cause headaches and stomachaches. Most health problems like these are not serious. They do not require us to go to a hospital.

2   A health clinic is a place where people can go if they have minor medical problems. It is not a private doctor's practice, which is very expensive. Likewise, it is not a hospital, which takes care of major medical problems. It consists of a group of doctors and nurses who have many offices in the same building. A visit to a health clinic is less expensive than a visit to a private doctor or a hospital.

3   Many universities have student health clinics (also called *health centers* or *health services*). All registered students can go there if they have minor health problems. For example, students go to the clinic if they have the flu, a bad cold, or an injury from a minor accident. Student athletes often use the university health clinic because they are sometimes hurt while playing their sports. Even the spouses of registered students can use the university health services.

4   University health clinics also take care of students with school-related health problems. Some examples of school-related health problems are stomachaches, headaches, and backaches. These problems are often caused by stress, when students feel tense and nervous during the school year. For example, at exam time, at the end of the term or the year, all students experience extra academic pressure. Too much academic pressure can cause health problems. Sometimes foreign students, however, also experience these problems during their first few months in a new country. The problems might be caused by stress from culture shock, by different food, and by not enough sleep. Students who feel sick because of culture shock or academic pressure can go to the university health clinic staff and services.

Health Clinic Staff

5   Who works at the student health clinic? Several kinds of professional people usually work there: physicians, physicians' assistants (these may be graduate medical students), counselors, and nurses. These doctors, counselors, and nurses take care of your physical health (your body) and your mental health (your mind). You can see one of them by making an appointment by phone or in person. You can also walk in to the clinic and wait your turn. If you have an urgent problem (an emergency), you can usually see a doctor without waiting.

C. Pearson Casanave

Checking in at the health clinic registration desk

Special Services and Fees

6   University health clinics usually have laboratories and X-ray units. For example, you can get a blood test at the health clinic. You might need to pay a small laboratory fee for the test. Or perhaps you think that you cracked a bone while playing a sport. In this case, you can go to the health clinic for an X-ray. An X-ray might be free or it might cost a small amount of money. These fees, however, are much lower than the fees at a regular doctor's office.

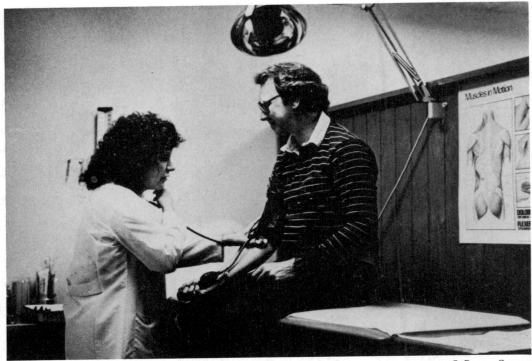

C. Pearson Casanave

Getting blood pressure checked by a health clinic nurse

7   Some health clinics have their own pharmacies. If a health clinic doctor gives you a prescription for some medication, you can get your prescription at the clinic pharmacy. The medications at health clinic pharmacies are usually less expensive than medications at regular pharmacies. If the clinic does not have a pharmacy, then you need to pay the full price at a regular pharmacy for your prescription.

What the Health Clinic Does NOT Do

8   Student health clinics do not take care of all of your health problems. For example, they do not take care of your teeth. For dental problems, you need to see a dentist. Similarly, the clinic does not test your eyes or give you glasses. You need to visit an optometrist or an ophthalmologist for eye problems. Finally, student health clinics do not take care of major medical problems. You can get the names of outside dentists and doctors from someone at the health clinic.

Staying Healthy

9   Health clinics take care of students who get sick. But students do not want to get sick. They want to stay healthy and stay *out* of the health clinic. Therefore, the clinic can give information to students about how to stay healthy. For example, health clinics usually have information about food and diet, about common illnesses, and about tension and stress (a common student health problem). This information is printed in individual brochures and pamphlets or in booklets. The brochures and booklets are free.

10   In conclusion, health clinics provide important services for students. Students help to pay for these services with their registration fees. If you are a student on a university campus, find out what the health center can do for you. If you do not have a health clinic on your campus, find out if there is one in your city. Learn about the health services that are available to you.

Comprehension Questions

Answer the questions orally or in writing.

1. Put a check next to the main ideas in the article. Do NOT check the details (small bits of information that support the main ideas).

    _____ The article tells us what health clinics do and do not do.

    _____ The spouses of registered students can visit the health clinic.

    _____ The article describes the staff at health clinics.

    _____ Students cannot get eyeglasses at the health clinic.

    _____ Students can get information about how to stay healthy at the health clinic.

    _____ The article discusses several important causes of health problems.

    _____ Students can get information about food and diet at the health clinic.

    _____ Health clinics are important places for students to know about.

2. We can learn from this article that _____ .
    a. health clinics are cheaper (less expensive) than regular doctors and pharmacies
    b. health clinics are more expensive than regular doctors and pharmacies
    c. the fees at health clinics, doctors' offices, and pharmacies are the same

3. True or false?
    a. All schools have health clinics.   T   F
    b. Health clinics are common at large universities.   T   F

c. Health clinics take care of minor health problems.	T	F
d. Health clinics take care of major health problems.	T	F
e. Students might need to pay a fee for blood tests and X-rays.	T	F
f. Medications are free at health clinics.	T	F
g. Stress from academic pressure and culture shock can cause health problems for foreign students.	T	F

EXERCISES AND FURTHER READINGS

A. Reference

Directions: Read the sentences. Some words are underlined. These words refer to a previous noun phrase. Write the noun phrase on the line.

1. For local students, community colleges are usually cheaper and more conveniently located than universities. Therefore, many students may attend them first before they go on to a university.

   THEM = _____

   THEY = _____

2. Many universities have student health centers, but our university doesn't have one yet. It is planning to build one next year.

   ONE = _____

   IT = _____

   ONE = _____

3. Some health centers give blood tests and X-rays. They do not cost very much.

   THEY = _____

4. Medications at health center pharmacies are less expensive than they are at regular pharmacies.

   THEY = _____

5. Students pay fees at the beginning of each school term. These usually include health services and student activity fees. If students don't pay them , they might not be able to complete their registration.

   THESE = _____

   THEM = _____

   THEY = _____

6. A university health center can take care of students with minor health problems. <u>It</u> cannot take care of <u>them</u> if <u>they</u> have major <u>ones</u> .

IT = _____

THEM = _____

THEY = _____

ONES = _____

7. Student health clinics take care of routine, minor medical problems. <u>They</u> do not take care of dental and eye problems. You need to see a dentist and an optometrist for <u>those</u> . Unfortunately, you will have to pay <u>them</u> a lot.

THEY = _____

THOSE = _____

THEM = _____

8. People can experience stomachaches and backaches from stress. If <u>they</u> can reduce <u>it</u> , these <u>problems</u> often disappear.

THEY = _____

IT = _____

THESE PROBLEMS = _____

B. Levels of Generalization

Read the groups of sentences. Write **G** before the most general sentence. Write **S** before the specific sentence(s). Write **MS** before the more specific sentence(s).

1. _____ Students commonly have two kinds of health problems.

_____ Colds and flu are examples of communicable diseases.

_____ These are communicable diseases and stress-related problems.

_____ Headaches and stomachaches are examples of problems that can be caused by stress.

2. _____ Some work at the information desk or in the office, and others examine patients.

_____ Many people work in a health clinic.

_____ Receptionists give out information and make appointments.

_____ Doctors examine people who are not feeling well and prescribe medications.

_____ Nurses take blood, test blood pressure, and generally assist doctors.

3. ____ The pressure from homework is daily.

____ The pressure from tests and quizzes is weekly or monthly.

____ Some pressures occur every day, others happen every week or two, and still others occur only at the end of an academic term.

____ The biggest pressure is from final exams and final papers.

____ All students are familiar with academic pressures.

C. Fact or Opinion

Directions: Read the statements. Circle **F** if you believe the statement is a fact. Circle **O** if it is someone's opinion.

	Fact	*Opinion*
1. Too much salt can cause health problems.	F	O
2. Food that is prepared with a lot of salt tastes better than food without salt.	F	O
3. Headaches are worse than stomachaches.	F	O
4. Stress and tension can cause headaches and stomachaches.	F	O
5. It is better to study in the morning than late at night.	F	O
6. Doctors in Europe are better than doctors in the United States.	F	O

D. Order

Directions: Read the list of health problems below. Put the list in order according to the seriousness of the problem (1 = most serious; 5 = least serious). Do you and your classmates agree about the order?

____ broken bone

____ cold

____ flu

____ headache

____ tension

E. Agree/Disagree

Directions: Read the statements. Circle **A** if you agree with the statement. Circle **D** if you disagree (do not agree) with the statement. Discuss your answers.

	Agree	*Disagree*
1. Every university should have a health center.	A	D
2. A good diet can prevent health problems.	A	D
3. Mental health is more important than physical health.	A	D
4. Students usually have poor eating habits.	A	D
5. Foreign students experience more tension than native students.	A	D
6. Students who are experiencing very bad culture shock should visit a school counselor or psychologist.	A	D

F. Getting Information from a Native Speaker

The article in this chapter mentioned some common health problems. It did not, however, mention any cures. How do you cure a stomachache? How do you treat a cold? Do your classmates agree with you? Do native speakers of English agree with you?

Directions: With your teacher, make a list on the blackboard of your class's ideas about how to cure each of the health problems below. Write some of the ideas on the lines.

Health Problem	*Ideas for Cures*
a headache	_____
	_____
a toothache	_____
	_____
a cold	_____
	_____
a stomachache	_____
	_____
a cut	_____
	_____

Now write the same list of health problems on another piece of paper. Ask a native speaker of English what a good cure is for each problem. If the native speaker answers, "Go to a doctor," ask, "Do you have a home remedy?" Write the native speaker's ideas on your paper. Then in class, compare all the native speakers' cures with your class's ideas. Do people from different countries have different ideas about cures for common health problems?

G. Read: At the Pharmacy

Rx   Take one tablet 3 times per day at mealtime first week; then one tablet daily second week until finished. Do not take on empty stomach. Consult physician in case of nausea or other side effects.[1] Caution: do not consume alcohol while taking this medication.

Answer the questions orally or in writing:

1. What do you think this is?

2. This information is not written in complete sentences. What words are left out? Can you rephrase it in complete sentences (orally or in writing)?

3. Do you think that these pills are strong or weak? Why do you think so?

4. What is one possible side effect of this medicine?

5. How many pills might be in this bottle when the patient gets it from the pharmacy?

6. Have you ever taken any strong medication? If so, did you have any side effects? What were they?

H. Read: "Professional" Advice

BEFORE YOU BEGIN: Read the list of symptoms. Look at the drawings. Match each symptom with the appropriate drawing by writing the symptom on the line under the drawing.

fever	headache	runny nose
sneezing	toothache	upset stomach
red and watery eyes		

---

[1]side effects (n, C, pl) = health problems caused by a medication

_____   _____   _____

_____   _____   _____

_____

Now read the following conversation to discover Alberto's health problem and Naomi's advice to him.

    Naomi: How are you feeling these days, Alberto?

    Alberto: Not so good, Naomi. My back still hurts a lot when I get up every morning.

    Naomi: You should do some back exercises in bed before you get up. That should take away the pain.

Naomi told Alberto to exercise—that was her advice to him. Have you ever asked someone for advice about a health problem? Have you ever given advice to someone with a health problem? You may have noticed that different people have different advice for the same health problem. Will you and your classmates give different advice to a person with a health problem?

   To find the answer to this question, first read the descriptions of health problems. Second, think of the best advice for each problem, and write your advice on the lines. Finally, compare your advice with your classmates' advice. Does their advice surprise you? Is it different from yours? Why do you think that advice about health is sometimes different?

1. Sue sneezes a lot and has a runny nose. She feels hot and cold and very tired. She has a fever. What should she do?

_____

_____

2. Debbie has a bad headache. The pain is the worst near her eyes. She also has an upset stomach. What should she do?

_____

_____

3. Mohammad has an upset stomach and a fever. His whole body aches. What should he do?

_____

_____

4. Judy has a toothache. When she drinks something cold, she feels a sharp pain in one tooth. What should she do?

_____

_____

5. Julio wakes up every morning with red eyes and a runny nose. He sneezes until about noon. Usually he feels fine in the afternoon and evening. What should he do?

_____

_____

I. Read: An Unhappy Patient

Dear Editor—

   I would like to comment publicly on the lousy service provided by our school's health center. I hope you publish this letter, because maybe somebody at the health center will read it and make some changes.

   First, it's almost impossible to see a doctor. Either the doctors are not there at all or they are all "busy." What are they busy with? Certainly not with students.

Second, if students go to the health center, they have to wait forever—sometimes more than one hour. Nobody should have to wait one hour for anything, but this is especially true for sick people.

Third, the medical students who work there don't know what they're doing. One time I went in for a sore muscle from a sports activity, and they took X-rays and blood tests. What a waste!

And finally, everybody's unfriendly there. If you feel sick when you go in, you feel sicker when you leave.

In my opinion, they should close the health center or do it right.

Unhappily,

A Dissatisifed Customer

Answer the questions orally or in writing.

1. Where might you read a letter like this one?

2. Who do you think wrote this letter?

3. How does this person feel about the health center in general?

4. Apparently some of the people who work at the health center are medical students. Why is this person unhappy with the medical students?

5. This person has several complaints about the health center. In your opinion, which complaint is the most serious? Which is the least serious?

6. Do you think that this person has chosen a good way to express his or her opinion? Do you think that the health center might change and improve because of letters like this one?

J. Read: Health Information at Your Fingertips

The Community Hospital of the Monterey Peninsula, in Monterey, California, has a telephone library. You can call a special telephone number and get tape-recorded information about many different health problems. First, read the information about Tel-Med. Then do the exercise.

TEL-MED

Health information available by calling

(408) 624-1999

Community Hospital of the Monterey Peninsula

Now you can call 624-1999 and get a tape-recorded message on a variety of health subjects in the privacy of your own home.

What It Is

Tel-Med is a telephone library of recorded health information tapes. Each tape is three to seven minutes long. The information is designed to help you stay healthy, help you recognize signs of illness, and help you adjust to a serious illness. Tape #429 describes in detail how Tel-Med was developed and how it works.

What It Is Not

Tel-Med tapes should not be used in an emergency or to find out what your illness is. If you have a health problem, you should call your doctor for diagnosis and treatment.
Hours to Call
Daily 9 a.m. to 8:30 p.m. For more information about Tel-Med, call (408) 649-1999 and ask for Tape #429.

How It Works

Just call 624-1999 and give the volunteer who answers the number of the tape you want to hear. When the tape is finished, your call will disconnect automatically. If you wish to hear the tape again, just call back. The subjects are listed in alphabetical order. Each subject is preceded by a tape number.

Directions: Find the tape numbers for the following health subjects. Find the subject category first. Work as quickly as possible. The first one is done for you.

Subject Category	*Subject*	*Tape Number*
blood	Blood Types and Factors	*146*
_____	Toothache, What to Do For	_____
_____	Effects of Drugs on Older People	_____
_____	Ulcers—What Should I Know?	_____
_____	Cigarettes and Heart Disease	_____
_____	Marijuana	_____
_____	Tension: Helpful or Harmful?	_____
_____	Low Salt Diets	_____
_____	Abortion	_____
_____	Influenza	_____
_____	Wisdom Teeth	_____
_____	Sore Throat	_____
_____	Skin Cancers	_____

Tel-Med®

Community Hospital of the Monterey Peninsula
Post Office Box HH Monterey, California 93940

Now you can dial 624-1999 and get a tape-recorded message on a variety of health subjects in the privacy of your own home. This free service is provided by the Auxiliary of Community Hospital Foundation in conjunction with the hospital's medical staff.

BIRTH CONTROL
886 Basal Body Temperature: Birth Control
54 Birth Control
55 Birth Control Pills
58 Diaphragm, Foam, Condom
68 Infertility
56 Intrauterine Devices
887 Mucus Method of Birth Control
57 The Rhythm Method
53 Tubal Ligation
1 Vasectomy

BLOOD
59 Donating Blood is Easy
91 Bleeding, Severe
1140 Blood in Urine
146 Blood Types and Factors

CANCER
6 Breast Cancer
523 Cancer of the Larynx
524 Cancer of the Mouth
176 Cancer of Prostate Gland
186 Cancer of the Uterus
183 Cancer's Seven Warning Signals
180 Cancer of the Colon and Rectum
184 Hodgkin's Disease
192 Leukemia
179 Lung Cancer
526 Mammography: Detection, Breast Cancer
188 Radiation Therapy for Cancer
185 Skin Cancers
5004 Sunburns—Skin Cancers can be Prevented

DENTAL
314 Bad Breath
313 Dentures, What You Don't Know Can Hurt You
307 Gum Disease—Seven Warning Signals
305 Malocclusion—Crooked Teeth
303 Plaque
311 Toothache, What To Do For
306 Wisdom Teeth

DIGESTIVE
78 Appendicitis: It's Still With Us
2 Bowel, "Normal"—What Is?
199 Colitis & Bowel Disorders
630 Diarrhea
662 Diverticulosis-Diverticulitis
4 Hemorrhoids
198 Hiatal Hernia
45 Indigestion
219 Laxatives: Use Them Rarely—If At All
196 Peptic Ulcer
44 Ulcers—What Should I Know?

DRUGS AND ALCOHOL
942 Alcoholism: The Scope of the Problem
136 Amphetamines & Barbiturates
142 Effects of Drugs on Older People
141 How New Medicines are Tested
140 How Safe are Drugs
134 LSD
137 Marijuana
138 Narcotics
135 PCP—Angel Dust

EMOTIONS (Also see Dial Dr. Brothers)
613 Anorexia Nervosa
616 Bulimia
726 Psychosomatic Illness: It's Not All In Your Head
727 Schizophrenia
405 Single Parent Family
33 Tension: Helpful or Harmful
432 Upset Emotionally? Help is Available
728 When Should I See A Psychiatrist?

EYES
472 Cataracts
473 Contact Lenses—Facts and Fallacies
9 Glaucoma
85 Pinkeye
474 Presbyopia—Need Glasses?
470 Seeing Spots and Floaters

FIRST AID FOR:
118 Animal Bites
121 Bee Stings
91 Bleeding—Severe
5034 Burns—Emergency Care
7019 Colds, Common
65 Chest Pains
111 Choking
103 CPR—Mouth to Mouth Resuscitation
610 Diabetes Emergencies
109 Epileptic Convulsions
108 Fainting
61 Fever, the Meaning of
563 Food Poisoning
116 Foot Problems
107 Heart Attack
7062 Poison Oak Rash
96 Poisoning by Mouth
149 Rape
94 Shock (Electric Shock 93)
99 Sprains
110 Unconscious Person

HEART DISEASE AND CIRCULATORY PROBLEMS
29 Atherosclerosis and High Blood Pressure
600 Cholesterol in Your Diet
21 Cigarettes and Heart Disease
23 Diet and Heart Disease
63 Heart Attack—Early Warnings
72 "Heart Failure"—What Is It?
28 How to Decrease the Risk of Heart Attack
25 Hypertension and Blood Pressure
30 Living with Angina Pectoris
5010 Mitral Valve Prolapse
26 Strokes
191 Varicose Veins

MUSCLES AND JOINTS
127 Arthritis—Rheumatism
129 Bursitis or Painful Shoulder
126 Gout
47 Leg Cramps, Aches and Pains
203 Osteoarthritis or Degenerative Joint Disease
128 Rheumatoid Arthritis
113 Tendinitis

NUTRITION
613 Anorexia Nervosa
616 Bulimia
603 Breakfast—Why Is It Important?
600 Cholesterol in Your Diet
601 Low Salt Diets
599 The Vegetarian Diet

PREGNANCY
24 Abortion
12 Am I Really Pregnant?
69 Artificial Insemination
881 Breastfeeding Your Baby
5 Early Prenatal Care
882 Emotional Feelings After Child Birth
5009 Fetal Alcohol Syndrome
66 Miscarriages—What Causes?
606 Nutrition in Pregnancy
32 Unwanted Pregnancy—Where Can I Get Help?
67 Warning Signs in Pregnancy

RESPIRATORY
576 Bronchial Asthma
581 Cough—Chronic
13 Emphysema
90 Hay Fever
584 Hyperventilation
38 Influenza
578 Pleurisy
7 Pneumonia
296 Sinus—Common Problems
70 Sore Throat
92 Strep Throat
583 Tuberculosis
40 Viruses—What Are They?

SKIN
172 Acne—The Heartbreak of Adolescence
83 Impetigo
518 Itching Skin
114 Plantar Warts and Moles
82 Psoriasis—Why the Mystery About It?
517 Scabies
87 Scleroderma

SMOKING
21 Cigarettes and Heart Disease

TEL-MED TAPE NUMBERS AND SUBJECTS

K. Read: Buying Medicine in Korea and in the United States

In this reading, Ho Hwan Yang, a graduate student from Korea at Stanford University, discusses some experiences he had when he first arrived in the United States. His discussion is in three parts. First, he tells us about a health problem he had and how difficult it was to buy medicine "over-the-counter" in the United States. He then compares buying medicine in Korea to buying medicine in the United States. He concludes with advice for other foreign students.

C. Pearson Casanave

"When I first came to the United States, I just couldn't sleep all night. I had very bad insomnia. Maybe this was culture shock. It was always accompanied by headaches and sometimes stomachaches.

"So I decided to buy some medicine to cure this problem. I went to some stores in Palo Alto, but I couldn't find what I was looking for. Of course, there were many medicines. But I didn't know what the dosage of the medicine was or how it would help my pain. I just couldn't find the correct medicine. Therefore, I just had to endure this pain. I kept awake all through the night. It was awful.

"In Korea, pharmacies sell all medicines—from antibiotics to tranquilizers—without a prescription. I know this is somewhat dangerous, but it is very convenient for me. In fact, when I was in Korea, I heard that it was very difficult to buy medicines in the United States. So I prepared some tablets to bring with me, for example antibiotics, pills for stomachaches, and some other medicines.

"As you can see, there is a big difference between Korea and the United States. Of course, there are some regulations about buying medicine in Korea. However, it is still possible to buy what you need in the drugstore. I don't want to say that the American system is wrong. In some ways it is better than the system in Korea. But right now, it is inconvenient for me. I need some specific tablets, and I can't get them without a prescription.

"Let me make some brief suggestions to other foreign students. First, and most important, don't get sick. Eat well and exercise properly. Second, if you have some pain—a headache or a stomachache—endure it. Too many tablets are not good for your health. The third and last suggestion—if you have some pain that you cannot endure, go directly to your doctor or to the student health center. The doctor will give you a prescription for the tablets you need. This way is difficult, I know, because the medical system is very different from the one in our countries. Maybe the best way is to go back to the first suggestion: Don't be sick, eat well, and exercise properly."

Discuss the following questions with your classmates.

1. Ho Hwan compares two systems for buying medications. In one system, people can buy almost all the medicine they need "over-the-counter," without a prescription from a doctor. In the other system, people need to see a doctor and get a prescription in order to buy strong medicines. In your opinion, what are the advantages and disadvantages of each system? What system do you have in your country?

2. Read Ho Hwan's advice to foreign students again. Do you agree with his advice?

THE WORD SECTION

A. Selective Reading: Cross Out Unrelated Word

Directions: Read the line of words. Cross out the word that does not belong with the other words. Work quickly.

1. nurses   dentists   teachers   physicians' assistants   doctors
2. health center   blood test   pharmacy   hospital   doctor's office
3. student   doctor   medication   photographer   businessman

4. stress   stomachache   diet   broken bone   headache

5. X-ray   fee   payment   cost   price

6. dentist   toothache   physician   ophthalmologist   pharmacist

B.   Selective Reading: Categorize

Directions: With another classmate, read the list of words. Put each word into one of three categories: **health problems, diagnoses,** or **medications/treatments.** If you do not know some of the words, ask your classmate or your teacher before you use a dictionary. Work quickly.

X-ray	headache	stress
aspirin	flu	blood test
cold	eye test	penicillin
stomachache	stitches	cough medicine
bandage	eye drops	antibiotic
broken bone	counseling	cancer
X-ray therapy	eye infection	cast

Health Problems	*Diagnoses*	*Medications/Treatment:*
_____	_____	_____
_____	_____	_____
_____	_____	_____
_____	_____	_____
_____	_____	_____
_____	_____	_____
_____	_____	_____

C.   Word Forms: Words Occurring with *ache* and *sore*

In this chapter, you saw that it is possible to combine a part of the body (e.g., *head*) with the word *ache* to form the new word *headache*. However, not all body parts can combine with the word *ache*.

Directions: With your teacher or with a native speaker of English outside class, look at the list of body parts below. Some of the words combine with *ache:* **headache.** Others combine with *sore,* but stay as two words: **a sore finger.** A few words combine both ways. Write all possible combinations on the lines. If a combination is not possible, write an X on the line.

	_____ *ache*	*a sore* _____
1. tooth		
2. arm		
3. foot		
4. stomach		
5. muscle		
6. hand		
7. knee		
8. back		
9. tongue		
10. thumb		
11. ear		

CHAPTER 8
Having Fun

PREREADING ACTIVITIES

Part 1: Identifying and Categorizing Activities

Look at the drawings on page 167. In each drawing, people are doing different activities.

a. As a class, identify the activity in each picture (Note: The words *picture* and a *drawing* refer to the same thing).

b. Next, sit with two or three classmates. In your group, organize the pictures into 3 categories. Think of a title for each category, and write the titles on the chart below.

c. Then list the pictures (by number and by activity) under the appropriate titles.

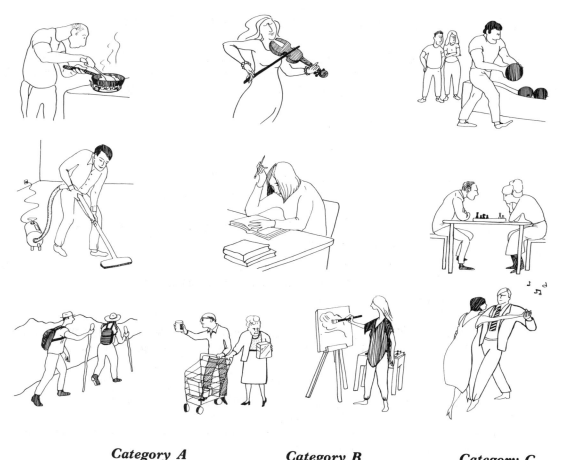

Category A	*Category B*	*Category C*
Title:	*Title:*	*Title:*

d. Next, compare your group's charts with the charts of other groups. How are the charts similar? Different?

e. Finally, discuss each group's reasons for dividing the pictures into categories. Are the reasons similar? Different?

Part 2A: Matching the Person with the Activity

What are some activities you enjoy? On a piece of paper, write three activities that are fun and enjoyable for you. Then write three activities that are not fun and enjoyable. Label each list. DO NOT WRITE YOUR NAME ON THE PAPER.

	Fun	*Not Fun*
EXAMPLE:	going to movies	playing golf
	playing tennis	swimming
	skiing	cleaning house

Next, sit with four or five classmates. Assign one person to be the group leader. The other group members need to give their lists to the leader.

Leader: Mix up all of the lists. Then give a list to each person in the group. Keep a list for yourself. (People should not have their own lists). Ask one person to read the information from his or her list out loud.

> EXAMPLE: "This person enjoys going to movies, playing tennis, and skiing. This person doesn't enjoy playing golf, swimming, or cleaning house. Who is it?"

The group needs to identify the person who wrote the list by matching the person with the list of activities. Then ask another person to read a list. Again, the group should try to match the person with the list of activities. Continue until all group members are matched with their lists. Finally, return the lists to their owners.

Question: How did you make your decisions? Do some of you like the same activities? Dislike the same activities?

Part 2B: Comparing Activities

You have six activities on your list from part 2A. Which of your activities do you enjoy the most? Write this activity on the line next to Number 1. Which of your activities do you enjoy the least? Write this activity on line next to Number 6.

Number 1 (the most fun): _____

Number 6 (the least fun): _____

Now read the statements below. If the statement describes your favorite (Number 1) activity, write 1 in the blank. If it describes your least favorite (Number 6) activity, write

6 in the blank. If it describes both activities, write 1, 6. If it does not describe either activity, write N/A (not applicable).

1. I usually do this activity alone. ____

2. I usually do this activity with other people. ____

3. My family also enjoys doing this activity. ____

4. I spend money when I do this activity. ____

5. Many Americans also enjoy this activity. ____

6. Many people in my home country also enjoy this activity. ____

7. I must travel to do this activity. ____

8. I must use special equipment (e.g. skiis, boat, guitar, paint, paper, etc.) to do this activity. ____

9. This activity is noisy. ____

10. This activity is quiet. ____

11. This activity is good for my health. ____

12. This activity is bad for my health. ____

13. This activity can be dangerous. ____

14. People need to practice a lot in order to be able to do this activity. ____

15. I must think a lot in order to do this activity. ____

When you finish, compare your answers with your classmates' answers. How are your answers similar? How are they different? What kinds of activities *in general* do you and your classmates consider to be fun? What can you learn about each other from this exercise?

Part 3: Survey and Predict

Read the list of key words. Then look at the title of the reading article on page 174. Look at the illustrations and the headings. Then check the topics below that you think will be important in this article.

____ How to avoid culture shock

____ Why people enjoy old movies

____ Different ways to have fun

____ How to earn money in your spare time

____ An old person's, a young person's, and a child's ideas about fun

Key Words

to have fun	**to sing**	**to play**
to mean	**to like (to do/doing**	**to chase**
to laugh	**something)**	
	to enjoy (doing	
	something)	

READING ARTICLE: Having Fun: Three Different Views

A.   HAVING FUN: THREE DIFFERENT VIEWS By Paragraph

1   An interviewer asked three different people the same question. These people gave different answers to this question. Read their answers below and try to guess the question.

Jean (20-year-old university student):   "Oh, I usually go to old movies like *Casablanca*. They're cheap entertainment."

Emiko (39-year-old laboratory technician):   "I go shopping with friends. Or sometimes we just go to a coffee shop and talk."

Paul (15-year old high school student):   "In the summer, I play baseball. In the winter, I go skiing as often as I can."

What was the question?

FROM THE ARTICLE: Jean, Emiko, and Paul ____ .
   a. are friends
   b. asked the same question
   c. had different answers to the same question

FROM THE ARTICLE AND THINK AHEAD: What did the interviewer ask Jean, Emiko, and Paul? _____

_____

---

2   The question that the interviewer asked was: "What do you do for fun?" Did you guess it? Of course, we can use other words to ask the same question. For example, these

questions all have about the same meaning as "What do you do for fun?": "What do you do to have fun?", "What do you like to do?", "What do you enjoy doing?", and "What do you do in your free time[1]?" The answers to these questions all have something to do with[2] fun. The word *fun* is very short (only 3 letters), but it can mean many different things. To Paul, fun means playing baseball or skiing. To Emiko, fun means shopping with friends. In other words, fun means different things to different people. In the next three paragraphs, you will discover some ways that three other people of different ages have fun.

THINK AHEAD: In the next few paragraphs, you will read about ___ .
   a. the author's definition of fun
   b. three different people's ideas about fun
   c. Paul, Jean, and Emiko

THINK AHEAD AND FROM THE ARTICLE: There are no other questions until almost the end of the article. However, after each section you will see a box with a question mark in it:

```
* * *  ?  * * *
```

When you see the boxed question mark ask yourself these questions:

FROM THE ARTICLE: *General:* Did I understand the last paragraphs? *Specific:* How does the person in this section have fun?

THINK AHEAD: What might come next in the article? If you did not understand a section well, go back and read it again.

Florence

3   Florence, a 73-year-old woman, had this to say about our interview question: "What do I do for fun? Well, that's a good question. When I was younger, I walked, hiked, and went horseback riding with my husband. Now my joints ache from arthritis, so I only

---

[1] free time (n, U, expr) = spare time or extra time

[2] to have something to do with (X) (v, expr) = to be connected or related to (X)

walk to the mailbox. Believe me, being seventy-three years old isn't always a lot of fun. When I wake up in the morning, it takes me twenty minutes to get out of bed. Not much fun.

4   "But you asked me about fun, not about my aches and pains. Let's see. When my bones hurt, I like to sit quietly and read. I read for several hours a day. If I take a few aspirin, I feel better, and then I like to visit friends. My husband and I have a lot of crazy friends. We get together with some of them once a week and play cards and Scrabble. My husband is a very funny[3] person, and he makes everybody laugh. We laugh until our stomachs hurt. He tries to cheat at cards while we are laughing, but we always catch him. Then we have another good laugh.

5   "I have fun with a couple of old girlfriends, too. We get together every Friday and sing. I play the piano. We even have a name for our group. We call ourselves 'The Golden Oldies.' Can you believe it? We aren't very good, but at least nobody is tone-deaf. We all have pretty good ears. And we sure do have fun!"

*** ? ***

Mark

6   Mark, a 30-year-old man, tells us: "I really like playing basketball, softball, and sometimes football. I mostly like team sports. In fact, playing team sports was the most enjoyable part of high school and college. But I like singing, too. I sing in the church choir every Sunday. I also like reading good books. I won't read a book that bores me. I can't understand why some people say, 'I read such and such a book and it was terrible.' I would never read a boring book unless someone forced me to read it. I guess that's one reason that I didn't like school, especially high school.

7   "One of my favorite activities is eating. I like having a good meal, and I like having it with someone. I like cooking, too, probably because I love to eat. I think I'm a pretty good cook. At least my friends and my wife tell me that. I also like going out to dinner—

---

[3]funny (adj) = humorous; capable of making other people laugh

that's fun. After a nice dinner at a restaurant, it's fun to go to the movies. I really like being with people. That's about all,[4] I guess."

```
*** ? ***
```

Scott

8   Scott, a 7-year-old boy, tells us this: "I like to play outside. I like to play cops and robbers, cowboys and Indians, and spaceman with the other kids in the neighborhood. I don't like to be the good guy. I like to be the bad guy. That's more fun. If I'm the bad guy, I can chase[5] everybody else and do whatever I want. I like to fight and wrestle.

9   "It's also fun to chase girls and cats. At school, I chase all the girls and pull their hair. I catch cats, too. I like to catch two cats and put them together and watch them fight. That's a lot of fun. But the most fun is to play tricks on the old man next door, Mr. Pickerton. He hates cats. So sometimes I catch a real ugly cat and put it in his house secretly. When he finds it, he gets real mad[6] and calls my mom.[7] It's real funny. But when my mom catches me, that's not fun. Ouch."

---

[4]That's about all. (expr) = I'm finished talking about this topic.

[5]to chase (v) = to run after (someone, something)

[6]real mad (adv + adj, expr) = very angry (informal)

[7]mom (n, C) = mother (informal)

$$*** \ ? \ ***$$

Conclusion

10   Florence, Mark, and Scott have fun in several different ways. Sometimes they have fun alone. For example, Florence and Mark enjoy reading, and Scott likes to chase cats. They also like to do things with other people. Mark plays basketball with his friends, Florence plays cards with her husband and their friends, and she sings with her girlfriends. Scott plays games with the neighborhood kids and chases girls at school. What do you like to do when you're alone? What do you enjoy doing with other people? Ask some of your friends—or your teachers—these questions. Talking about fun is usually a lot of fun!

B.   HAVING FUN: THREE DIFFERENT VIEWS   Complete Reading

1   An interviewer asked three different people the same question. These people gave different answers to this question. Read their answers below and try to guess the question.

Jean (20-year old university student): "Oh, I usually go to old movies like *Casablanca*. They're cheap entertainment."

Emiko (39-year old laboratory technician): "I go shopping with friends. Or sometimes we just go to a coffee shop and talk."

Paul (15-year old high school student): "In the summer, I play baseball. In the winter, I go skiing as often as I can."

What was the question?

2   The question that the interviewer asked was: "What do you do for fun?" Did you guess it? Of course, we can use other words to ask the same question. For example, these questions all have about the same meaning as "What do you do for fun: "What do you do to have fun?", "What do you like to do?", "What do you enjoy doing?", and "What do you do in your free time?" The answers to these questions all have something to do with fun. The word *fun* is very short (only 3 letters), but it can mean many different things. To Paul, fun means playing baseball or skiing. To Emiko, fun means shopping with friends. In other words, fun means different things to different people. In the next three paragraphs, you will discover some ways that three other people of different ages have fun.

Florence

3   Florence, a 73-year-old woman, had this to say about our interview question: "What do I do for fun? Well, that's a good question. When I was younger, I walked, hiked, and

went horseback riding with my husband. Now my joints ache from arthritis, so I only walk to the mailbox. Believe me, being seventy-three years old isn't always a lot of fun. When I wake up in the morning, it takes me twenty minutes to get out of bed. Not much fun.

4   "But you asked me about fun, not about my aches and pains. Let's see. When my bones hurt, I like to sit quietly and read. I read for several hours every day. If I take a few aspirin, I feel better, and then I like to visit friends. My husband and I have a lot of crazy friends. We get together with some of them once a week and play cards and Scrabble. My husband is a very funny person, and he makes everybody laugh. We laugh until our stomachs hurt. He tries to cheat at cards while we are laughing, but we always catch him. Then we have another good laugh.

C. Pearson Casanave

5   "I have fun with a couple of old girlfriends, too. We get together every Friday and sing. I play the piano. We even have a name for our group. We call ourselves 'The Golden Oldies.' Can you believe it? We aren't very good, but at least nobody is tone-deaf. We all have pretty good ears. And we sure do have fun!"

Mark

6   Mark, a 30-year-old man, tells us: "I really like playing basketball, softball, and some-times football. I mostly like team sports. In fact, playing team sports was the most enjoy-able part of high school and college. But I like singing, too. I sing in the church choir every Sunday. I also like reading good books. I won't read a book that bores me. I can't understand why some people say, 'I read such and such a book and it was terrible.' I would never read a boring book unless someone forced me to read it. I guess that's one reason that I didn't like school, especially high school.

Diane Williams

7   "One of my favorite activities is eating. I like having a good meal, and I like having it with someone. I like cooking, too, probably because I love to eat. I think I'm a pretty good cook. At least my friends and my wife tell me that. I also like going out to dinner—that's fun. After a nice dinner at a restaurant, it's fun to go to the movies. I really like being with people. That's about all, I guess."

Scott

8   Scott, a 7-year-old boy, tells us this: "I like to play outside. I like to play cops and robbers, cowboys and Indians, and spaceman with the other kids in the neighborhood. I don't like to be the good guy. I like to be the bad guy. That's more fun. If I'm the bad guy, I can chase everybody else and do whatever I want. I like to fight and wrestle.

Martha Casanave

9   "It's also fun to chase girls and cats. At school, I chase all the girls and pull their hair. I catch cats, too. I like to catch two cats and put them together and watch them fight. That's a lot of fun. But the most fun is to play tricks on the old man next door, Mr. Pickerton. He hates cats. So sometimes I catch a real ugly cat and put it in his house secretly. When he finds it, he gets real mad and calls my mom. It's real funny. But when my mom catches me, that's not fun. Ouch."

Conclusion

10   Florence, Mark, and Scott have fun in several different ways. Sometimes they have fun alone. For example, Florence and Mark enjoy reading, and Scott likes to chase cats. They also like to do things with other people. Mark plays basketball with his friends, Florence plays cards with her husband and their friends, and she sings with her girlfriends. Scott plays games with the neighborhood kids and chases girls at school. What do you like to do when you're alone? What do you enjoy doing with other people? Ask some of your friends—or your teachers—these questions. Talking about fun is usually a lot of fun!

Comprehension Questions

Answer the questions orally or in writing.

1. This article discussed _____ .
   a. differences between young people and old people
   b. different ways that people enjoy their free time
   c. how to talk to different kinds of people

2. The authors _____ .
   a. gave you their opinion about the best way to have fun
   b. talked with a total of six different people about having fun
   c. told you how they (the authors) have fun
   d. probably do not have much fun

3. What are some of the ways that each person in the article has fun? Try to answer without looking back at the article.

   Florence likes to _____

   _____

   Mark likes to _____

   _____

   Scott likes to _____

   _____

4. What do Florence and Mark have in common?

They both enjoy _____

5. True or False?
  a. Scott enjoys getting into trouble.   T   F
  b. Mark didn't enjoy school because the books were boring.   T   F
  c. Florence does not have much fun anymore because she is too old.   T   F

6. Put a check next to the main ideas in the article. Do not check the details.

____ Mark enjoys team sports.

____ People can have fun alone or with others.

____ Florence and Mark both like to read.

____ There are many different ways to have fun.

____ Florence, Mark, and Scott probably don't know each other.

____ Scott is a troublemaker.

7. Think of some old people that you know (friends or relatives). What do they do for fun? Do their activities seem fun to you?

8. Think of some small children that you know. What do they do for fun? Do all small children enjoy getting into trouble? Only boys? Did you have fun getting into trouble when you were a child?

9. The people who were interviewed in this article have fun in many different ways. Make a list of the things that they do for fun that you also enjoy.

_____

_____

_____

_____

EXERCISES AND FURTHER READINGS

A. Reference

Directions: Read the sentences. The underlined words and phrases refer to a noun phrase or a verb phrase that came earlier. Write the noun phrase or the verb phrase on the line.

> EXAMPLE: Angelina enjoys playing tennis, but David doesn't . He prefers to watch tennis games on TV.
>
> DOESN'T = *doesn't enjoy playing tennis*
> HE = *David*

1. Racquetball and handball are popular indoor sports. Businessmen often play these games during their lunch hours.

   THESE GAMES = _____

2. The VCR (Video Cassette Recorder) is becoming more and more popular. This machine allows people to watch movies in their homes. Nevertheless, some people still like to watch them in movie theaters.

   THIS MACHINE = _____

   THEM = _____

3. If you see Houssam, please tell him to bring some ice to the dinner party tonight. If he doesn't , we will not have it in time to make the drinks.

   HIM = _____

   HE = _____

   DOESN'T = _____

   IT = _____

4. In order to win the game of Blackjack, the players' two cards should total 21. If the player doesn't have 21 but the dealer does , the dealer wins. This game is popular at gambling casinos.

   DOES = _____

   THIS GAME = _____

5. People read books for many reasons. <u>One</u> is that <u>they</u> are required to read <u>them</u> for a class. Reading for this reason isn't always fun. <u>Another</u> is that <u>they</u> simply enjoy reading. If <u>they</u> <u>do</u> , reading can be a very enjoyable activity.

ONE = _____

THEY = _____

THEM = _____

ANOTHER = _____

THEY = _____

THEY = _____

DO = _____

B. Grammatical Word Groups: Identify

Directions: Look at the word group in parentheses. Underline the grammatical word groups that have a similar grammatical structure.

1. (cheap entertainment)   Emiko's answer   excellent food   sing together   sunny weather   go downtown

2. (on the hill)   guess the question   have a quartet   in the house   for fun   through the tunnel

3. (to laugh)   to guess   to my mind   to Jean's answer   to the store   to have fun   to chase

4. (asked the best question)   as often as I can   wrote a long letter   my mother saw   tried a new recipe   you guessed it

C. Fact or Opinion

Directions: Read the statements. Circle **F** if you believe the statement is a fact. Circle **O** if you believe the statement is an opinion. *Note:* Some of the statements are from the reading. Other statements are general. Discuss your answers in class.

	Fact	*Opinion*
1. It is fun to watch old movies.	F	O
2. Baseball and basketball are team sports.	F	O
3. Baseball and basketball are interesting sports to watch and play.	F	O
4. Old people do not enjoy walking and other physical exercise.	F	O

5. Young children who are troublemakers will grow up to be trouble-makers as adults.   F   O

6. The word *fun* means different things to different people.   F   O

D.   Grammatical Word Groups: Read

Directions: Read the following paragraph, which is divided into grammatical word groups, three times: first with vertical spacing, then with horizontal spacing, and finally with normal spacing. Read as quickly as you can.

1.   Vertical

Western Movies

It's a lot of fun
to watch old Western movies.
The stories
are always very predictable.
There are "bad guys" and "good guys."
Sometimes the bad guys are cowboys.
In that case,
they always wear black hats and vests
and ride dark horses.
Sometimes the bad guys are Indians.
In that case,
they wear feathers and warpaint
and ride painted horses.
The Indians always speak English.
The good guys,
on the other hand,
wear white hats
and ride white horses.
There is always
a lot of chasing, shooting, and fighting.
Of course,
the good guys always win.

2. Horizontal

It's a lot of fun   to watch old Western movies.   The stories   are always very predictable.   There are "bad guys" and "good guys."   Sometimes the bad guys are cowboys.   In that case,   they always wear black hats and vests   and ride dark horses.   Sometimes the bad guys are Indians.   In that case,   they wear feathers and warpaint   and ride painted horses.   The Indians always speak English.   The good guys,   on the other hand,   wear white hats   and ride white horses.   There is always   a lot of chasing, shooting, and fighting.   Of course,   the good guys always win.

3. Normal Spacing

It's a lot of fun to watch old Western movies. The stories are always very predictable. There are "bad guys" and "good guys." Sometimes the bad guys are cowboys. In that case, they always wear black hats and vests and ride dark horses. Sometimes the bad guys are Indians. In that case, they wear feathers and warpaint and ride painted horses. The Indians always speak English. The good guys, on the other hand, wear white hats and ride white horses. There is always a lot of chasing, shooting, and fighting. Of course, the good guys always win.

E. Agree/Disagree

Directions: Read the statements. Circle **A** if you agree. Circle **D** if you disagree. Discuss your answers in class.

	Agree	*Disagree*
1. Husbands and wives should enjoy the same activities.	A	D
2. Men are better at playing team sports than women are.	A	D
3. Little boys and little girls should play with different kinds of toys.	A	D
4. Children these days watch too much TV.	A	D
5. Teachers should not force students to read books that the students don't like.	A	D

F. Read: A Board Game

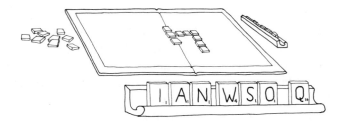

Directions: Read the following selection. Then, with two or three other students, answer the questions as best you can.

HOW TO BEGIN:

1. Turn all letters face down.
2. Each player chooses seven letters. Put letters on rack.

HOW TO PLAY:

1. First player forms a word from his or her letters and puts word on board. Word on board must be placed up and down or across. Diagonals not permitted.
2. First player counts score by adding points from each letter of the word. Player then draws new letters so total on rack is again seven.
3. Next player forms new word from existing word on board by adding letters from his or her rack. New word must be up and down or across. Diagonals not permitted.
4. Second player counts score, then draws new letters to total seven.
5. Each player continues in the same manner until all possible letters are used.

HOW TO END:

1. Game ends when no letters remain on the table and no player can form a word on the board.
2. Players' scores are totalled. Player with highest score wins.

Answer the questions orally or in writing.

1. Where do you think this selection is from? What does it describe?
2. How many players do you think can play this game?
3. Do you think that players in this game can use a dictionary? Why or why not?
4. Have you ever played a game like this?
5. Do you know what the name of this game is?
6. Do you think this game sounds like fun?

G. Read: Animal Play

BEFORE YOU BEGIN: In this article, the word *zoologist* is used several times. Without using your dictionary, try to guess the meaning as you read.

1   Probably everyone has seen baby animals such as kittens and puppies play. These young animals certainly seem to be having fun. They chase each other, tumble and wrestle, chase their tails, and play with objects such as string, balls, and sticks.

2   Do all animals play? What is the purpose of their playing? These are questions that zoologists ask. In order to answer these questions, we must first agree on a definition of *play*. This is difficult, since even zoologists do not agree on a definition.*

3   For this discussion, we will use our common sense to decide what play is. From our experience, we can say that play is a pleasurable activity that humans and animals do for fun. This activity often imitates[1] serious and purposeful activities, but it doesn't achieve a serious goal. Of course, humans often play very seriously. Professional and amateur sports are examples of serious, elaborate[2] play.

---

*Edward O. Wilson, *Sociobiology* (Cambridge, MA.: The Belknap Press, 1975), p. 164.

[1] to imitate (v) = to copy or mimic a behavior

[2] elaborate (adj) = complicated, detailed

Reasons Why Animals Play

4   Why do animals play? The most important reason is probably to learn some of life's serious activities. Adult animals, for example, need to look for food, to fight, to look for a mate,[3] and to get along with[4] other animals of their kind. Young animals can practice these important life activities by playing. Through play, they can imitate hunting for food, fighting, courting[5], and socializing. They can learn how to control their movements, how to interact with their environment, and how to interact with other animals in their group.

Which Animals Play

5   Not all animals play. In fact, zoologists tell us that only vertebrates[6] play, and among them, primarily the higher vertebrates. For example, insects, fish, and reptiles do not play, but most mammals[7] do, especially when they are young. In general, we can say that highly intelligent animals play more than less intelligent animals. In other words, the higher the intelligence of the animal, the more elaborate the play will be.

6   The chimpanzee is the most intelligent of the nonhuman mammals. This primate plays in an elaborate, complicated way. Chimpanzees chase each other, wrestle, and invent[8] a variety of games. Only humans play in a more complicated way. The play of chimpanzees and humans is a way of having fun. But it is also a way for these intelligent animals to be creative—to interact with their environments in new ways. Perhaps human creativity in music, art, and science begins as a kind of play.

---

[3]a mate (n, C) = a partner or companion of the opposite sex

[4]to get along with (v, expr) = to be compatible with (someone); to relate to (someone) without fighting

[5]to court (v) = to try to win a mate

[6]vertebrates (n, C, pl) = animals that have a spine (backbone)

[7]mammals (n, C, pl) = vertebrates that feed their young with milk

[8]to invent (v) = to create; to make something new

Answer the questions orally or in writing.

1. What is a zoologist? _____

2. According to the article, which animal probably plays the most? The least? Put a number from one (the most) to ten (the least) next to each animal. You will need to guess. Compare your choices with your classmates' choices.

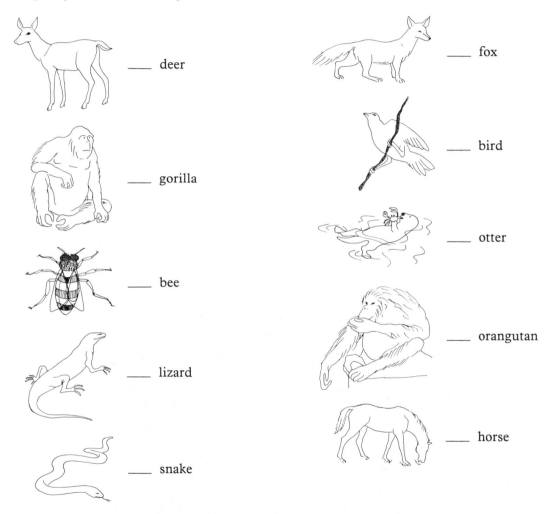

_____ deer

_____ gorilla

_____ bee

_____ lizard

_____ snake

_____ fox

_____ bird

_____ otter

_____ orangutan

_____ horse

3. In the following sentence from the article, the word *do* is underlined. This word functions like a verb. However, it has no real meaning here, because it is a substitute for another verb in the sentence. What verb does it replace?

"For example, insects, fish, and reptiles do not play, but most mammals <u>do</u> ."

DO = _____

4. True or false? The author believes that the only purpose of animal play is to have fun.   T   F

5. Dogs are more intelligent than cats. According to this article, which of these two animals plays in a more elaborate way? Do you agree?

6. The author says that animals play in order to learn important life activities. Do you agree or disagree? Do human children play for the same reason? Give some examples of how children play.

H. Read: The Playful Sea Otter

Directions: Read the questions first. Then read quickly in order to find the answers. Do not read more than you need to (you can read more carefully later).

Questions:

1. What is a sea otter? _____

2. Where do sea otters live? _____

3. What are *pups*? _____

4. Where is one place that sea otters live in captivity (= not in the ocean)? _____

_____

Richard Bucich

A California sea otter floats in kelp in one of its infrequent moments of rest.

1   Sea otters, the most playful of the marine[1] mammals, live in the cold ocean water along the coasts of California, British Columbia, Alaska, and the Soviet Union. They spend a great deal of[2] their time grooming[3] and looking for food. But sea otters are also very social animals. They live in small groups. The groups might be all males or they might be mixed-sex (male-female) groups. Some of the females might have pups with them.

Somersault

Tumble

Wrestle

2   Otters interact with other otters in their group in a variety of ways. One way that they interact is by playing. Usually they play in pairs. They chase each other, tumble and wrestle, and leap in and out of the water. They turn somersaults and roll over and over each other. The males sometimes imitate fighting. The females carry their pups, who seem to enjoy the ride. Pups tumble and wrestle with each other.

3   In some places, such as the Monterey Bay Aquarium in Monterey, California, a few sea otters are kept in captivity. These captive sea otters do not need to spend a lot of time looking for food, since food is given to them. Therefore, they can spend more time interacting and playing. Tourists never get tired of watching these amazing marine mammals who seem to have so much fun.

4   But are the otters really playing? Or are they conducting important life activities? Some sea otter specialists believe that otters *must* behave this way in order to stay alive—to stay warm, to eat, to take care of their coats, and to behave correctly in their social group. What looks like play to the human eye might be survival behavior for the otter.

IF YOU ARE INTERESTED IN SEA OTTERS, READ THE ARTICLE AGAIN MORE CAREFULLY. When you finish, discuss the following questions with your classmates.

1. From the last article ("Animal Play"), this article, and your own knowledge, try to guess why sea otters play. (Discuss your ideas with your classmates. Any ideas are fine. Even zoologists don't have a clear answer.)

2. Do you think that sea otters are intelligent animals? Try to explain your answer.

3. Sea otters eat a great deal of food—about 20 percent of their body weight every day. Can you think of a reason why they eat so much?

---

[1]marine (adj) = living in the ocean

[2]a great deal of (adj, expr) = a lot of

[3]to groom (v) = to take care of hair, fur, skin; to make hair, fur, and skin neat and tidy

I. Read: "Junk Mail"

BEFORE YOU BEGIN: As you read this letter, think about whether it is serious or funny.

PICTURE PERFECT PIZZA PALACE

Y O U ' R E   A   W I N N E R ! ! ! ! !

Dear **MR. AND MRS. BLACKSTONE,**

CONGRATULATIONS! OUR COMPUTERS HAVE CHOSEN YOUR NAME AS ONE OF THE WINNERS IN OUR BIG PICTURE PERFECT PIZZA PRIZE GIVEAWAY! LAST YEAR, **MR. J. SOLOMON** *FROM YOUR HOME TOWN* WAS OUR GRAND PRIZE WINNER. HE WON $5,000,000,000 (IN COUPONS GOOD TOWARD THE PURCHASE OF PICTURE PERFECT PIZZAS ANYWHERE IN THE WORLD). YOU, TOO, CAN BE A BIG WINNER, **MR. AND MRS. BLACKSTONE,** BECAUSE YOU HAVE THE SAME CHANCE OF WINNING AS **MR. SOLOMON** DID.

BUT IF YOU'RE NOT THE GRAND PRIZE WINNER, YOU ARE GUARANTEED TO BE A WINNER ANYHOW! HERE ARE SOME OF THE OTHER PRIZES THAT YOU CAN WIN (AND REMEMBER, YOU WILL WIN ONE OF THESE PRIZES):

ONE COMBINATION PICTURE PERFECT PIZZA PER WEEK FOR THE NEXT 5 YEARS

100 BOXES OF PICTURE PERFECT FROZEN CHEESE PIZZAS

50 TINS OF PICTURE PERFECT PREMIUM ANCHOVIES

10 COUPONS FOR A BEVERAGE OF YOUR CHOICE AT ANY PICTURE PERFECT PIZZA PALACE ANYWHERE IN THE WORLD

A LOVELY PICTURE PERFECT PIZZA BUTTON

A COLORFUL PICTURE PERFECT PIZZA BUMPER STICKER

HOW TO COLLECT YOUR PRIZE, **MR. AND MRS. BLACKSTONE?** JUST TAKE THIS LET-TER TO ANY PICTURE PERFECT PIZZA PALACE, ORDER ONE LARGE COMBINATION PIZZA AND THE PRIZE IS YOURS! DON'T WAIT, **MR. AND MRS. BLACKSTONE!** COL-LECT YOUR PRIZE TODAY! YOU MIGHT BE THIS YEAR'S GRAND PRIZE WINNERS!

Answer the questions orally or in writing.

1. Who do you think sent this letter?

2. How many people do you think received the same letter?

3. How much money might Mr. and Mrs. Blackstone win?

4. What do Mr. and Mrs. Blackstone need to do in order to collect their prize?

5. What prize do you think they will win?

6. What benefit does the pizza company get from this contest?

7. Have you ever received a letter similar to this one? If so, what did you do with it?

8. Why do you think this kind of letter is called "junk mail"?

9. Do you think that this example of junk mail is funny? If so, what makes it funny?

THE WORD SECTION

A. Selective Reading: Underline Examples (from sentences)

Directions: Read the sentences. Underline all of the words that are examples of the word in parentheses.

EXAMPLE: (furniture) Florence likes to read in a comfortable <u>chair</u>.

1. (activity) Older people often enjoy walking or driving. Another favorite pastime is playing cards with friends.

2. (day of the week) Restaurants are crowded on Friday and Saturday nights. In contrast, many restaurants are closed on Mondays.

3. (holiday) Families often visit relatives during school and religious holidays such as Thanksgiving, Christmas, New Year's, and Easter.

4. (entertainment) Tourists who visit New York City like to shop, go to movies and shows, and eat at famous restaurants. They also enjoy visiting some of New York's many museums.

5. (food) The cake was gone when I finally arrived at the party, so I ate the candy and the nuts.

6. (sports)   Some businessmen keep fit by playing racquetball or handball during lunch hours. They might also play tennis and golf on weekends and on business trips.

7. (medical problem)   Emiko went to the health center to get some medicine for her toothache. While she was there, she saw a young man with a broken leg brought in on a stretcher.

B. Selective Reading: Underline Examples (from paragraphs)

Directions: Underline all of the examples of the words in parentheses in the following paragraphs. Do not worry if you don't understand the exact meaning of all the words. Read quickly.

(specific occupations)   (ways of relaxing or having fun)

In a nine-to-five job, workers (both blue collar and white collar) leave for work in the morning and come home in the evening at the same time every day. Secretaries, construction workers, businessmen, and sales clerks, among others, all have regular, predictable work schedules. These workers can easily plan what to do after work and on weekends to relax. They can watch TV regularly. They can play cards and board games with friends and relatives on a regular basis. They can go bowling, have picnics, and go to church and club activities on the weekends.

Other professions do not follow such a regular nine-to-five schedule. Doctors and surgeons, for example, often work very early and very late. They may be called away from parties, dinners, and even night-time sleep in order to attend to emergencies. These interruptions are normal for them. Many teachers, professors, and researchers have irregular schedules, too. They also tend to bring their work home with them. The work of preparing for classes, correcting papers, and solving a research problem does not end at 5:00.

Sometimes people in the medical and teaching professions have difficulty finding time to relax. They need to make a concerted effort to spend time with their families, go to movies, read for pleasure, go out to dinner, and socialize with friends. Like some business executives, they can easily become "workaholics."*

---

*"workaholics" (n, C, pl) = people who work too much (from *alcoholic,* a person who drinks too much)

C. Word Forms: -er Ending (nouns; adjectives); *more* Comparatives; Negative Prefixes *un-*, *in-*, and *im-*

1. Review

Directions: Write the meaning of each word in the blank. Look for prefixes and suffixes that you know. (Review the Word Section in Chapters 2 and 5 if necessary.)

EXAMPLE: teacher *a person who teaches*
   unhappy *not happy; sad*

uncomfortable _____

lecturer _____

unfamiliar _____

photographer _____

unfriendly _____

2. Comparatives: Another Use for *-er; more* + Adjective

The ending *-er* is added to short adjectives (and adverbs) to compare two things.

EXAMPLE: Health center fees are **lower than** regular doctors' fees.

In this example, what two things are compared?

1. _____

2. _____

What adjective is used? _____

What word follows the comparative form of the adjective? _____

In general, we add *-er* to short adjectives (one syllable, sometimes two syllables) to make the comparative form. The adjectives *good* and *bad* are irregular. Their comparative forms are *better* and *worse* (than). With longer adjectives, and with adjectives that end in *-ed,* we make the comparative form with *more.* Look at the examples on the next page.

This book is **more interesting than** that magazine.

However, the photographs in the magazine are **better than** those in the book.

I am **more bored** by television **than** by radio.

(Note: The negative comparative forms of adjectives are *not so/as* [*adjective*] *as* and *less* [*adjective*] *than*.)

Directions: Read the list of adjectives. First, count the syllables in each one. Then, on another piece of paper, write sentences that compare the items in parentheses. The sentences should express your opinion, so change the order of the items if necessary.

Adjective	*Number of Syllables*	*Items to Compare*
high	____	(a grade of A / a grade of C)
old	____	(my father / my mother)
sensitive	____	(men / women)
active	____	(old people in my country / old people in the United States)
good	____	(food in my country / food in the United States)
sick	____	(people with colds / people with flu)
expensive	____	(movies in my country / movies in the United States)
nervous	____	(new students / continuing students)
strong	____	(American coffee / coffee from my country)

3.   Getting Information from a Native Speaker: The Negative Prefixes *un-, in-,* and *im-*

In Chapter 2 (The Word Section) you practiced the prefix *un- (=* not). The prefixes *in-* and *im-* can also mean *not:*

*in*sensitive = not sensitive

*im*possible = not possible

(But note: The prefix *in-* can also mean *in* or be a part of another prefix or word: *inflamed, influential, inch.* Use context to figure out if the meaning is *not.*)

Directions: Read the list of adjectives. We can make a negative form of these adjectives by adding the prefix *un-*, *in-*, or *im-*. Fill in the blanks with the negative forms that you are certain about. Then, outside class, ask a native speaker of English to give you (orally) the forms that you are not sure about. Write the forms in the blanks. Later, compare your list with your classmates' lists. Are the lists the same? Discuss any differences or patterns that you find.

Adjective	*Negative Form*	*Adjective*	*Negative Form*
possible	_____	correct	_____
convenient	_____	married	_____
fortunate	_____	polite	_____
active	_____	social	_____
controlled	_____	intelligent	_____
important	_____	complicated	_____
probable	_____	creative	_____
expensive	_____	perfect	_____
experienced	_____	professional	_____
predictable	_____	injured	_____
painted	_____	proper	_____
hurt	_____	complete	_____
interesting	_____	personal	_____

D. Analogies

We can sometimes explain or describe something, such as a feeling or an activity, by using an analogy.

> EXAMPLE: The pain in my arm is very sharp. It is **like a knife.**
> EXAMPLE: To some people, American football is **a little like a free-for-all fight.** To other people, it is **like a board game.**

Directions: Read the incomplete sentences on the left. Find an appropriate analogy from the list on the right and complete the sentences. (You can also write your own analogy.) More than one analogy might be appropriate.

1. A bad stomachache can feel like

_____ .

2. The pain in my back is like

_____ .

3. A good movie is like

_____ .

4. Playing chess is like

_____ .

5. When I have a cold, my head feels like

_____ .

6. While my sister was skiing, she fell. Her leg broke like

_____ .

7. Falling in love is like

_____ .

a stick

problem-solving

an adventure

fire

a knife

a heavy rock

flying

psychological war

an explosion

_____

_____

_____

E. Word Association

Directions: Read the list of words. What does each word make you think of? Write as many words as you can. Work quickly. Then compare your words with your classmates' words. Do the words below make you and your classmates think of similar things?

1. fun _____

2. medicine _____

3. old people _____

4. boring _____

5. marriage _____

F. Getting Information from a Native Speaker

In the prereading activities for this chapter, you discovered what your classmates like to do for fun. In the main reading article, you discovered what Florence, Scott, and Mark do for fun. What do the Americans around you do in their free time? Do a simple survey. Outside class, ask one or more Americans one of these questions:

1. What do you do for fun and relaxation?

2. What do you do in your free time?

Make a list of the answers. Write down who the person is (for example: young male student; middle-aged female professor; elderly male landlord). Later in class, make a list of everyone's answers. Discuss your findings in class.

Appendix:
Key Vocabulary Words

(from footnoted items and key words lists)

Word or Phrase *(part of speech as used in text)*	Page
above (adv)	**32**
above all (expr)	**73**
accident (n, C)	**142**
adjustments (n, C, pl)	**64**
advice (n, U)	**48**
to agree (v)	**40**
airplane (n, C)	**48**
amateur (n, C)	**90**
to arrest (v)	**105**
a.s.a.p. (expr)	**119**
at a discount (expr)	**51**
athletic (adj)	**115**
aunt (n, C)	**24**
to avoid (v)	**50**
bathrooms (n, C, pl)	**72**
to be friends (v, expr)	**115**
to be in one's 40s (v, expr)	**118**
to be sad (happy, worried, homesick, serious) (v + adj)	**24**
both (adj and pn)	**118**
breakfast (n, C)	**115**
broadcast (n, C)	**60**
brother (n, C)	**24**
businessman (n, C)	**24**
to call (v)	**23, 24, 27**
camera (n, C)	**90**

Word or Phrase *(part of speech as used in text)*	Page
to chase (v)	**170, 173**
cold (n, C)	**142**
common sense (n, U, expr)	**116**
compatible (adj)	**115**
correspondence (n, U)	**132**
to court (v)	**186**
cousin (n, C)	**24**
to criticize (v)	**82**
darkroom (n, C)	**119**
depressed (adj)	**79**
to develop (v)	**90**
differences (n, C, pl)	**115**
difficult to use (expr)	**90**
dinner (n, C)	**115**
distinguishing characteristic (n, C, expr)	**1**
to double (v)	**40**
to dress up (v)	**82**
easy to use (expr)	**90**
eccentric (adj)	**132**
e.g. (abbr = for example)	**1**
elaborate (adj)	**185**
to elope (v)	**132**
emigrants (n, C, pl)	**26**
to enjoy (doing something) (v)	**170**
family (n, C)	**24**

Word or Phrase (part of speech as used in text)	*Page*
father (n, C)	24
fee (n, C)	142
to feel (get, be) sick (v)	142
flu (n, U)	142
for instance (expr)	50
to forget (v)	48
free time (n, U, expr)	171
friends (n, C, pl)	24
funny (adj)	172
to get along with (v, expr)	186
to get married (v)	115
to get used to something (v, expr)	82
grandparents (n, C, pl)	24
GRE (Graduate Record Exam) (n, C, abbr)	128
a great deal of (adj, expr)	189
greedy (adj)	39
to groom (v)	189
to have fun (v)	170
to have something to do with (X) (v, expr)	171
headache (n, C)	142
huge (adj)	27, 60
I don't care for _____ (expr)	117
to imitate (v)	82, 185
information (n, U)	142
interesting (adj)	48
to invent (v)	186
it doesn't matter (expr)	105
kids (n, C, pl)	31
laboratory (n, C)	142
to laugh (v)	170
to leave home (v)	24
letter (n, C)	115
light (n, U)	94
light (adj)	94
to like + n (v)	115
to like to + v (v)	115, 170

Word or Phrase (part of speech as used in text)	*Page*
to lose (v)	48
to love (v)	115
love (n, U)	115
lunch (n, C)	115
major (adj)	68, 142, 143
mammals (n, C, pl)	186
marine (adj)	189
mate (n, C)	186
to mean (v)	170
medication (n, C)	142
minor (adj)	142
mom (n, C)	173
mother (n, C)	24
musician (n, C)	115
nephew (n, C)	24
newcomer (n, C)	79
niece (n, C)	24
to omit (v)	113
ordinary (adj)	94
parents (n, C, pl)	24
party (n, C)	24
pets (n, C, pl)	71
pharmacy (n, C)	142
photo/photograph (n, C)	90
photography (n, U)	115
plane (n, C)	48
to play (v)	170
plenty of (expr)	60
plus (adv)	117
prescription (n, C)	142
presents (n, C, pl)	31
problem (n, C)	48
professional (n, C)	90
to promise to + v (v)	24
real mad (adv + adj, expr)	173
reason (n, C)	48
relatives (n, C, pl)	24
restrooms (n, C, pl)	72

Index